"Access to artistic life must be one of the mainstays for developing and affirming social inclusion for all young people" See page 7

Summary 2

Section 1

Section 2

Section 3

Section 4

Section 5

Section 6

Appendices

Summary

A summary of the *How Much?* project and its outcomes

The *How Much?* project aimed to test how the mix of programming, price and promotion influences young people's attendance of Sheffield Theatres. Funded through the Arts Council's New Audiences scheme, the project ran between September 1998 and December 1999.

The report illustrates that through a combination of demography, seating capacity, and programming opportunities, Sheffield Theatres was in a unique position to carry out audience development with an emphasis on the impact of pricing policies targeted at young people. The report goes on to argue that *How Much?* has strengthened Sheffield Theatres' claim to continue with such work, building on the impressive results of the initial funding period. [Section 1 acts as an introduction and outlines the rationale for the research and artistic development strands of the *How Much?* project. The section concludes with a timetable of project activity].

The information that forms the basis of this report came from 4 sources:

▶ Sheffield Theatres' business plan, identifying the potential for audience development in various market segments, including young people

▶ Sheffield Theatres' programming information and box office data, tracking the sales and marketing history of 32,000+ *How Much?* transactions

▶ research on the attitudes and behaviour of young theatre attenders (sample size 1,000), non-attenders (554) and gatekeepers (15 teachers, lecturers, youth workers etc.) conducted by The University of Sheffield and Sheffield Hallam University

▶ an evaluation of the organisational and external impact of the artistic development strand - D2K and 23:59

Although the original remit of *How Much?* was to investigate price sensitivity among young audiences, programming and promotion were soon recognised as elements of equal importance to that of price. The project's overarching concern became the influence of the mix of programming, price and promotion on young people's attendance of Sheffield Theatres. [Section 2 outlines Sheffield Theatres' initial thoughts on implementation, areas for research and the project's reporting framework. The section is included as a baseline from which to measure the project's progress].

Programming

21 productions were programmed under the *How Much?* banner [See page 34]

▶ 32,000+ tickets were sold to young people for these productions between September 1998 and November 1999 [See Section 3].

▶ the proportion of young people in Sheffield Theatres' audience rose from 7% prior to the project to an average of 41% on *How Much?* productions. (The national average is 16%) [See Section 3].

▶ programming for a younger audience can lead to the alienation of traditional theatregoers (Mojo). But these traditional theatregoers can be enthused to attend the same productions as young people if an artistic vision is clearly communicated (Angels in America) [See Section 3].

▶ on average, 29% of the audience for *How Much?* productions were new attenders, the great majority of whom (93%) felt 'encouraged to return to Sheffield Theatres' [See Section 4.1].

▶ modern drama, comic drama and stand-up comedy were consistently cited as attractive programming by young people

▶ there were significant gender and age differences in programming deemed 'attractive' by the non-attenders sample [See Section 4.2]

▶ young people are notional risk-takers - they enjoy the idea of risk but will only attend if their peers are prepared to join them [See Section 4].

▶ the 'risk' of powerful emotional involvement can be counterbalanced by the spectacle of live performance, programming well-known productions or casting familiar (from TV) actors [See Section 4].

▶ commissioning a new play (23:59) and programming it, unseen, into the Crucible during the autumn 1999 season was a high-risk decision - the nature of which was valued by young people and undervalued by some critics [See Section 5].

Price

How Much? productions were priced at £3.50, except Mojo (£5) and 23:59 (£4.50), for young people aged 16-24.

▶ 54% of the young people questioned spent £45 or more each week on leisure activities. However, a significant minority (28%) spent less than £20 each week

▶ for attenders and non-attenders price was not an absolute constraint to theatre attendance, but the uncertainty of what they would get in return for their money resulted in theatre being more susceptible to financial reasons for non-attendance than other leisure activities

▶ although price was only one factor in choosing whether or not to attend the theatre, ticket discounts were listed as a major incentive by attenders (86%) and the perception that Sheffield Theatres was too expensive was the greatest constraint expressed by non-attenders (48%) and gatekeepers

▶ attenders' perception of theatre-going being expensive reduced by 15% as the *How Much?* project progressed

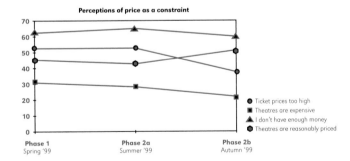

Perceptions of price as a constraint

● Ticket prices too high
■ Theatres are expensive
▲ I don't have enough money
● Theatres are reasonably priced

Phase 1 — Spring '99
Phase 2a — Summer '99
Phase 2b — Autumn '99

▶ 58% of attenders stated (retrospectively) that they would have been prepared to pay more for their ticket

▶ c66% of attenders and non-attenders expressed a willingness to pay between £3 and £9.99 for a theatre ticket

Effectiveness of marketing communications by age

16 - 24

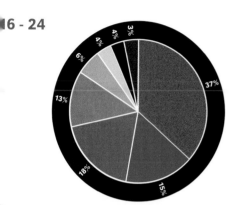

All ages

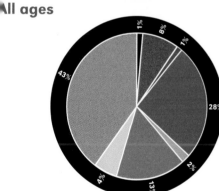

- How Much? print
- Season Brochure
- Flyer
- Poster
- Newspaper
- Other
- Radio
- Word of mouth
- Direct mail

Promotion

The *How Much?* project was promoted through specific season brochures, leaflets, posters, radio and the new Sheffield Theatres website [see Section 3].

- ▶ word of mouth was the most significant source of information for young people
- ▶ a brochure giving full production details generated 69% more sales than a flyer with only basic details of the same productions
- ▶ the new Sheffield Theatres website attracted 6,952 hits in the *pilot phase*, rising to 17,113 in *phase 1*
- ▶ young people's response to direct mail was, on average, 25% lower than that of Sheffield Theatres' core audience. Sourcing new mailing lists generated an increase of 6% in the impact of direct mail on young people
- ▶ new partnerships, such as audience development activities with the Centre for HIV and Sexual Health, and Sheffield and District Afro-Caribbean Community Association (SADACCA), can reassert the centrality of theatre in initiatives to promote community development and social inclusion
- ▶ focus group-led design needs to be mediated by professional marketing input

The future

[See Section 6]

- ▶ *How Much?* ticket discounting and other incentives are being continued through the young person's element of Sheffield Theatres' Square Circle membership scheme. The scheme currently has more than 1,200 members aged 16-26
- ▶ Sheffield Theatres' relationship with The University of Sheffield and Sheffield Hallam University continues. Six areas for further research have been identified
- ▶ partnerships forged during *How Much?* are being maintained through joint initiatives
- ▶ lessons from the project are being integrated with general marketing activity
- ▶ findings from the *How Much?* project are being used to support funding applications for sustainable audience development work with young people
- ▶ the value of undertaking youth audience development work in Sheffield's crucible of demography, seating capacity and programming opportunities has been strengthened by the impressive results of the *How Much?* project.

05

Section 1 | How Much?
New audiences for Sheffield

Section 1

New audiences
for Sheffield

Making theatre count for young people

by Angela Galvin,
marketing and development director, Sheffield Theatres

*Print image for **Mojo** written by Jez Butterworth*

06

How Much? Section 1
New audiences for Sheffield

The challenge of attracting a new generation of theatregoers is not unique to Sheffield. Most theatres acknowledge the need to build audiences of the future. Many arts organisations have conducted research and implemented audience development projects. The *How Much?* project was devised in response not only to the government's pledge, in the Labour Party manifesto, to support wider access to the arts, but also to Sheffield Theatres' need to build new audiences.

▶ The city of Sheffield has a higher proportion of 16 to 24-year-olds than the national average, yet Sheffield Theatres has a lower proportion of young audiences than the national average.

▶ Young people in Sheffield earn, on average, around £1,500 less than they spend each year.

▶ Sheffield Theatres has three auditoria in which to programme and produce a wide range of live performance.

▶ Sheffield Theatres has the seating capacity to enable low-price tickets to be targeted at low-income groups without excessively undermining box office income.

Sheffield's population structure, Sheffield Theatres' ability to programme a broad range of performance in different settings, and financial support from the Arts Council of England's New Audiences fund all combined to create fertile ground for an imaginative project building on the experience of others and contributing new insights to the vital area of developing new audiences.

Why focus on young people?

The debate about young people's engagement with theatre predates the Daily Telegraph's comment (left), but it is a view that encapsulates the issues:

▶ Are we in a situation where young people have to make a stark choice - either videos, films and the internet or theatre?

▶ Are today's young people inherently uninterested in plays - or can that interest be re-awakened or even stimulated for the first time?

'Regional theatres are failing to cater for the young, who grew up with videos, films and the internet. They [young people] are unimpressed by drama and have little knowledge of plays.'

Daily Telegraph, February 14 2000.

07

Section 1 | How Much?
New audiences for Sheffield

The *How Much?* project has not asked young people to give up videos, film, the internet or other pursuits. Instead, we would argue that engagement with live theatre is a basis for interpreting and enriching the experience of these forms of media. The value of live theatre is, we believe, its tension, immediacy and uniqueness. Unlike technological entertainments, theatre is not heavily mediated - its points of identification are strong, alive and human. As such, theatre can have a humanising effect - access to live performance can enhance social interaction. It can give greater understanding of issues outside our own experience. Access to this artistic life must be one of the mainstays of the longer-term agenda for development and affirmation of social inclusion for all young people.

The youth market is of interest to politicians, educationalists and commercial businesses as well as arts organisations. We all have something to 'sell' - citizenship, the value of education, the latest product or, in our case, the benefits of visiting Sheffield Theatres. But selling more tickets is not our only imperative. We believe passionately that there is a process of engagement and emotional involvement in live performance that benefits not only the artists but also the audience. The *How Much?* project was not about inducing young people to the theatre simply to increase our box office takings on a particular production. Its aim was to enable greater numbers of young people to experience the emotional benefits of theatre-going. We knew that some of these young people would choose not to visit the theatre again. Of course, we hoped that some of them would choose to become regular theatregoers - our audiences of the future. Chiefly though, we were adamant that none of them should feel excluded from visiting the theatre again.

The city and its young people

Sheffield is the fourth largest city in England, with a strong sub-regional role. The city has unique demographic profiles incorporating not only the postcodes with the highest concentration of professionals in England (S10 and S11), but also an overall population where 64.4% live in areas at the lower end of the 'ACORN' classification (reflecting the city's strong working class tradition). Almost 1.2 million people live in around 500,000 households within a 30-minute drive-time of the city centre. In the Arts Council of England's Area Profile Data (1997), more than 300,000 of these people said they had attended a theatre in the past 12 months.

The proportion of 16 to 24-year-olds in Sheffield is above the national average. With two universities and one of the largest further education colleges in Europe, the student population is now in the region of 50,000. This student population reflects the demographic shape of the wider population. The University of Sheffield has been characterised as one of the 'elite' universities. It receives considerable research funding and recruits mainly from upper-middle class sections of the UK

population. Sheffield Hallam University emphasises its excellent track-record of students finding employment and concentrates on recruiting from a broader range of social backgrounds (and ages). According to recent surveys, students in these two universities have an average annual income from all sources of £3,615 against an average expenditure of £5,091. So money and budgeting are an issue.

Sheffield and its theatres

Sheffield Theatres is also unique. Since 1991, one management has run the complex of three theatre spaces (Crucible, Studio and Lyceum). No one had attempted previously to run a regional producing theatre (Crucible) alongside a commercially orientated receiving venue (Lyceum). Lastly, the Studio space provides Sheffield with an impressive and exciting range of auditoria, and the challenge of filling 2,400 seats.

The Crucible.
This was built in 1971, with a thrust stage and seats for 980. It offers a programme of touring and Sheffield Theatres' homegrown productions. Views on the building and ambience tend to range from pleasantly informal to shabby. The Crucible also has an unbroken history of investment in its education department's work, through theatre in education, youth theatre, and other young people's theatre projects.

Studio.
This is part of the Crucible complex. It offers flexible space, seating up to 400 in the round. It hosts the internationally renowned Music in the Round chamber music festivals and small-scale drama.

The Lyceum.
This is a traditional proscenium stage, built in 1897, with seats for 1,080. It was closed in 1969, and re-opened after massive refurbishment in 1991. It is a 'receiving house', offering mainly toured-in work, ranging from West End musicals, Royal National Theatre and Royal Shakespeare Company shows, to opera, and also ballet.

Like many regional theatres, Sheffield saw a decline in audiences from the early 1990s. A new approach to marketing and programming has stemmed the flow, leading to increased attendance (by 7%) and box office income (17%) in 1998/99.

▲ | *Illustrations:*
| *The Crucible, Studio and*
| *Lyceum Theatres.*

09

Section 1 | How Much?
New audiences for Sheffield |

However, early in 1998, research indicated that although general audience numbers had stabilised, the proportion of under-25s attending the theatres had fallen to approximately 7% and was well below the national average (16%) suggested by Target Group Index (TGI) figures.

Previous 'taster' initiatives have had some success in attracting younger audiences, but Sheffield Theatres has not had the resources to convert first-time attenders to become regular theatregoers. Retention of audiences and making theatre-going a habit is a key issue.

Designing the research

Sheffield Theatres was interested in exploring ways in which artistic, programme and audience development could combine to make the theatres more attractive to young people - increasing audiences while maintaining box office income and artistic integrity. Our aim was to design an explicit, precise and systematic research project, which could provide real world recommendations.

If the research was to influence Sheffield Theatres' strategic decisions in these areas, it needed to be well-designed and clear. At a very early stage (May '98) we were approached by Peter Taylor, professor of leisure management at the Management School of The University of Sheffield, offering to lend his expertise. We eventually 'signed up' with Prof. Taylor and his colleagues at the Leisure Industries Research Centre, a collaboration between The University of Sheffield and Sheffield Hallam University.

We feel that the involvement of academics lent a valuable external perspective to *How Much?* The tension between the academics' striving for controlled investigation and our own persistent introduction of new variables and inconsistencies was also illuminating. Critically, the researchers had to take account of the fact that we are a working organisation facing a real issue that affects our current and future prosperity.

The research element of *How Much?* built on learning from a wide range of arts organisations and audience development projects. However, it was essentially 'action research' in the sense that our everyday practice responded to feedback and incorporated findings throughout the project's lifetime. Sheffield Theatres needed to experience the process of formulating our own questions and getting our own answers in order to learn from the project. We are confident that this

approach has given the research more integrity. By describing the process we have also made the findings more useful for other arts organisations.
[See the introduction to the surveys, Section 4].

Using the research

Our aim was for the research to enable us explicitly, precisely and systematically to identify how the mix of programming, price and promotion influences young people's attendance of Sheffield Theatres. In fact, some of the findings were contradictory or inconclusive and require another stage of analysis before conclusions and recommendations could be converted to policy.
[See further research recommendations, Section 4].

Throughout the project, there was some pressure from our main funder to produce results in terms of the volume of ticket sales. Given that *How Much?* was initially funded for 12 months, this emphasis on quantity and instant results inhibited our ability to build relationships requiring a more patient and long-term approach. In particular, our work with socially excluded young people (for example, young offenders, unemployed) and those reached through employers and statutory agencies was affected. Relationships in these areas, where the quality of engagement is arguably more important than the numbers of tickets sold, are still being pursued.

D2K and 23:59

Our original proposal included two innovative aims that sat outside a simple market research framework:

▶ to involve young people in the production of artistic material relating to the *How Much?* project

▶ to create a piece of theatre specifically targeted at young people

These strands were characterised as 'artistic development' - a balance to the audience development element of the scheme.

The first of these aims was to become D2K - a group of young artists selected to work on the project and develop their skills in writing, photography and performance. It was envisaged that two artists in residence (a performance artist and a graphic artist) would nurture them.

▲ *Illustrations:*
23.59 - *a play created for young people*
Sheffield Theatres' information point at the
Forum shopping centre.

11

Section 1 | How Much?
New audiences for Sheffield |

The theatre piece evolved as 23:59, written by Nicola Baldwin and staged in the Crucible in November 1999. [See Section 5 for a fuller description and evaluation]

Funding partners

The *How Much?* project was dependent on funding received from the Arts Council of England's (ACE) New Audiences scheme. In return for generous financial support, ACE required information on

- ▶ numbers of performances covered by the scheme
- ▶ the proportion of the audience coming from the target age group (16 - 24)
- ▶ gross box office potential and box office achieved
- ▶ numbers of additional activities, such as workshops and pre-show discussions.

Other partners in the scheme fell into three broad, and not necessarily exclusive, categories:

- ▶ those who wanted to support investment in new audiences
- ▶ those who wanted to support investment in artists
- ▶ those for whom young people are also a target market.

Of these, the first tended to attract financial support whereas the second and third generated enthusiasm, ideas and support in kind. [See Appendices for list of partner organisations].

Timetable

May - August 1998

- ▶ Sheffield Theatres admitted to ACE's New Audiences scheme
- ▶ steering group formed
- ▶ project objectives set: marketing and research strategies produced
- ▶ *pilot* season programmed
- ▶ *pilot* ticket prices set

Pilot phase: September - November 1998

Central Sheffield Theatres' production:
Twelfth Night, directed by Michael Grandage

- ▶ targeted promotions started
- ▶ project co-ordinator appointed (October)
- ▶ quantitative research: box office data and questionnaires
- ▶ qualitative research: discussion groups
- ▶ *phase 1* programmed
- ▶ *pilot phase* ticket prices reviewed and *phase 1* ticket prices set
- ▶ analysis of early findings. Clarification of marketing and research objectives

Phase 1: December 1998 - April 1999

Central Sheffield Theatres' production:
Mojo, directed by Deborah Paige

▶ quantitative research: as *pilot phase*
▶ qualitative research: Focus groups and in-depth interviews
▶ official project launch (February)
▶ sales and information point opened at The Forum (young people's shopping centre)
▶ artistic development objectives discussed
▶ dramaturg appointed
▶ **D2K** young artists' project started
▶ playwright for production to be aimed at young people (23:59) appointed
▶ comparison of *pilot data* and *phase 1* data
▶ *phase 2a* programmed

Phase 2a: May - August 1999

Central Sheffield Theatres' production:
Angels in America Part one: Towards the Millennium,
directed by Phil Willmott

▶ continued outreach and research based on analysis of *pilot* and *phase 1*
▶ theatre staff attend awareness-raising workshops on access for young people
▶ **D2K** artists stage their production, Trashed, in Crucible Studio
▶ input to programming, pricing and promotions for future seasons
▶ 'play offs'- a 48-hour writing project, takes place in Crucible
▶ pilot young people's membership scheme launched

Phase 2b: September - December 1999

Central Sheffield Theatres production:
23:59 by Nicola Baldwin, directed by Sarah Frankcom

▶ **D2K** exhibition at National Centre for Popular Music
▶ qualitative research: focus groups and in-depth interviews
▶ quantitative research: final phase of questionnaires
▶ dramaturg's contract ended
▶ project co-ordinator's contract ended
▶ universities collated research findings
▶ first draft of final project report and recommendations

March 2000

▶ production of final report and recommendations

▲ | *Illustration:*
Print image for **Angels in America Part One: Towards the Millennium.**

13

Section 1 | How Much?
The view from the starting line

Section 2

The view from the starting line

The following account, written by Angela Galvin, Sheffield Theatres' marketing and development director, in August 1998, indicates the perspective and the aspirations that informed the early stages of the *How Much?* project. Its inclusion here offers a baseline from which the progress of the project can be assessed.

Print image for **Twelfth Night** *written by William Shakespeare*

Background

Sheffield Theatres Trust has received £300,000 as part of the Arts Council's New Audiences initiative. The Trust's proposal, *How Much?* has a particular but not exclusive focus on 16-24-year-olds. Its aims can be summarised as:

▶ exploring the impact of ticket pricing on access to theatre performances

▶ finding ways in which 'access' ticket pricing can co-exist with static revenue support from public or private funding sources (i.e. how can we cut ticket prices when we need to be making more money from box office?)

▶ developing artistic, programming and community partnerships to support enhanced access

Our own market research shows that younger audiences are most sensitive to price. Over the past 12 months we have attracted a younger audience by targeting standby tickets at students. There are three other discounts which apply to young people - students, youth and music stage pass holders and education groups. Current sales patterns on these discounts provide a fixed point from which to measure the impact of *How Much?* activities.

Implementation

The first of the *How Much?* activities will be to apply a one-price ticket targeted at 16 to 24-year-olds across selected shows already programmed for the autumn 1998 season. The autumn *How Much?* price has been fixed at £3.50 so that it compares favourably with Sheffield cinema pricing. This price will apply to 16 to 24-year-olds and schools parties on the following autumn shows:

▶ Moving Voices

▶ Popcorn

▶ A Clockwork Orange

▶ Twelfth Night

▶ Rambert Dance Company

Box office staff will not be asking customers for a birth certificate - the 'policing' of the scheme will be in targeting marketing communications which reflect the emotional and economic triggers for that age group.

Promotion

The marketing department has also produced an education briefing for schools and colleges. This has been published under the title of the highly successful schools newsletter - Trip Out - formerly produced by South Yorkshire Arts Marketing.

▲ *Illustration:*
Trip Out - *Sheffield Theatres'*
newsletter for schools.

15

Section 2 | How Much?
The view from the starting line

SYAM no longer have the resources to produce the newsletter, so we have 'bought' the title and, hopefully, the goodwill attached to it.

An interim *How Much?* logo was designed in May to flag up the project in the autumn brochure. This logo has now been adapted and will be used on specific print and advertising campaigns targeted at young people for distribution from September onwards. The *How Much?* funds have enabled us to strike a deal for the design and maintenance of a website for Sheffield Theatres, with a particular focus on promoting the project. The site will be hosted by Sheffweb (part of Sheffield Newspapers) and will be the hub of a daily updated city guide to be launched in the first week of September '98. Our address: www.sheffweb.co.uk/sheffieldtheatres.html.

Initially, our site will be based on the season brochure, with a specific *How Much?* element to go live at a later date. Available information indicates that there is a 50/50 split between home and work usage of the web and internet services and that this usage is predominantly by men (c90%) in their 20s. However, these user-patterns are changing, particularly amongst students who have free access through college. The website will give us access to audiences that are not traditional theatre ticket purchasers either by age or gender.

These marketing communications will highlight the low prices and the elements of the productions that might have a particular appeal to young people. For Twelfth Night and the Rambert Dance Company there will also be targeted marketing activity to encourage schools from less well-off communities to take advantage of the unprecedentedly low prices.

Context and choice

Recent research in Sheffield showed that young people are more likely to attend classical drama than any other theatre form. This finding may have much to do with context - seeing theatre-going as an activity organised through school or college - in which case classical drama is probably what they will be *taken* to see rather than what they might *choose* to see if they were aware of the full range of productions. The autumn 1998 season across the Crucible and Lyceum theatres combines productions with an appeal to younger audiences - Popcorn, A Clockwork Orange with those which will attract educational parties - Twelfth Night, Rambert Dance Company. Moving Voices, targeted at people with learning disabilities, will enable us to explore wider issues of accessibility. The Rambert Dance Company introduces access to an artform other than drama. Sheffield Theatres' unique ability to programme touring and repertory productions across three very different venues provides an opportunity to test the notion of context and choice, albeit on a fairly superficial level at this stage.

Sustainability

The project planning process now underway has financial, time and strategic dimensions - how much money have we got and how much extra do we have to raise? How much can we sensibly achieve in a 12-month period, and how much of that achievement will be sustainable beyond the original project? How much will the project be integrated with our business plan?

A steering group aided by the project workers appointed in autumn 1998 will address these issues and the lessons from this *pilot phase*. By that time, Sheffield Theatres expect to have started the process of raising match funding of around £100,000 - an element of the funding package which could be a key to the project's sustainability.

How Much? has generated a great deal of enthusiasm and interest locally. We have already identified or been approached by artists, schools, target communities, local media, academics etc. with whom we can develop the 'non-price' artistic, programming and partnership objectives throughout 1999. We are also pursuing partnerships with venues that our research has shown to be popular print outlets for young people.

Above all, *How Much?* is not simply a ticket discounting exercise. One objective is to identify the extent to which ticket pricing is a factor when young people choose their leisure activities, but we do not want to entice a new generation into the theatre and then leave them dangling when the project funding runs out. We need the relationships forged during the project to extend beyond a one-night stand, so sustainability is also a key objective. The New Audiences money and additional funding enables us to experiment with audience development, marketing activity and programming in a way which will place *How Much?* in a continuum of sustainable activity rather than a one-off project vacuum.

Pilot phase pricing and research framework

The research framework for the *pilot phase* is underpinned by three objectives:

1. to establish the relationship of product to target audience
2. to establish the level of price sensitivity in the target audience
3. to investigate the contexts in which the options for theatre attendance are set

Other areas of monitoring and analysis will cascade from these objectives. The learning from each component of the *How Much?* project will be incorporated in subsequent pricing, platform and marketing initiatives.

Reporting framework

To ensure some consistency in the reports generated from different sources, we have agreed the following 'reporting framework'. All analysis should refer back to the overarching question:

HOW DOES THE MIX OF PROGRAMMING, PRICE AND PROMOTION INFLUENCE YOUNG PEOPLE'S ATTENDANCE OF SHEFFIELD THEATRES?

This big question can be broken down into the following manageable units:

1. How many people go to what and why?
2. Who goes to what and why?
3. Do lower ticket prices 'grow' attendance?
4. What marketing communications are effective?
5. How important are platform/education events?
6. What is the nature of our relationship with new audiences? Is it sustainable?
7. How will the above influence Sheffield Theatres' strategic market position?
8. Can/could this initiative sustain itself without government funding?

▲ *Illustration:*
Skateboarder Neil Chester helps launch **How Much?**

17

Section 3 | How Much?
The medium and the message

Section 3

The medium and the message

Sheffield Theatres'
How Much?
programming and marketing activities

October 1998 to November 1999

Peter Lee-Wilson, Jack Tanner and Alan Westaway in **Mojo** *written by Jez Butterworth*

In describing Sheffield Theatres' programming and marketing decisions, this section tries to indicate where particular lessons were learned and, where appropriate, how our approach to the *How Much?* project changed as a result of appraising our activities.

The account is broadly in chronological order, following the project phases from the *pilot* (autumn 1998) through to *phase 1* (spring 1999), *phase 2a* (summer 1999) and *phase 2b* (autumn 1999). However, there are two issues arising from the *pilot phase* which underpin the other activities and are dealt with separately:

▶ the overall objectives
▶ targeting

Modifying the overall objectives

The aims of the project were modified following the *pilot phase* (autumn 1998) in order to incorporate what had been learned. Chiefly, we resisted the temptation to combine too many audience development priorities under one project umbrella. We soon realised that some sections of our 16 to 24-year-old audiences required a greater level of engagement over a longer period than that for which *How Much?* was funded. In business terms, it was the difference between an objective to 'grow' young people's attendance quickly, and one to improve the quality of our relationships with key audiences over time. For example, the *pilot phase* included a production (Moving Voices) targeted at young people with learning disabilities. Although building stronger links with people with disabilities remains a priority, we felt this work should develop outside the *How Much?* project, with greater freedom from the pressure to deliver measurable results. [1]

Following the *pilot phase* then, the project's aims were condensed into five headings:

1. To explore the importance of programming, ticket price and promotion as a practical issue in access to theatre performances for the broad population - and especially for the young (16-24).
2. To find realistic ways in which theatre can use ticket pricing, programming and promotion to encourage greater cultural diversity amongst its audiences.
3. To investigate ways to ensure the longer-term sustainability of the project.
4. To develop working partnerships with arts, community and other groups in order to enhance access.
5. To publish a study of the project, with practical recommendations.

1 E.g. Disability awareness sessions have been held for all staff in conjunction with the award-winning company of disabled actors, Full Body and the Voice. Our relationship with the company continues to develop.

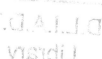

19

Section 3 | How Much?
The medium and the message

Targeting

The 16-24 age group selected itself as the target for the *How Much?* project, in that it was the age group identified by the Arts Council of England for its New Audiences scheme. From our previous research, we were aware that the eight years covered by this target group contained great diversity. For example, targeting those at the lower end would potentially overlap with marketing already targeted at young people through schools and youth groups [see Gatekeepers, Section 4]. The status of those at the upper end could range from students through to the unemployed or even the relatively well-paid.

One of the key aims of *How Much?* was to ensure that the project was perceived as being inclusive of anyone aged 16-24. With 50,000+ students in Sheffield, as a group they will clearly make up a significant proportion of young audience numbers. However, we have learned not to become over-dependent on our student population as the main youth market. Although the volume of students is immense, it is a largely transient population, with considerable seasonal fluctuations. During the first phases of the project, we also targeted other key segments.

Market segments within the 16-24 age range:

▶ 16-18 still at school
▶ 16-18 who had left school and were working
▶ 18-24 who were university students or graduates
▶ 18-24 who were at work
▶ those on government training schemes
▶ further education college students
▶ young unemployed people

Segmentation by frequency of attendance:

▶ non attenders *(have not attended the theatre at all in the past year)*
▶ infrequent attenders *(have attended the theatre 1-3 times in the past year)*
▶ frequent attenders *(have attended 4+ times in the past year)*

Although clear about differences in age and status, at the earliest stage of defining our target markets we were not explicit about another key variable in the 16 to 24-year-old age group: independence. We discussed 'context and choice' in the original project outline (see section 2), referring to the difference between being taken to the theatre, for instance as a member of a school party, and choosing to go independently. But as the research data grew, the importance not only of financial independence but also the ability to make independent choices grew more evident.

Financial independence has an obvious impact on the ability to buy tickets. The level of independent decision-making addresses not only the perception of young people's theatre attendance being predominantly organised by parents, schools or youth groups, but also the issue of peer pressure, 'I'd go but none of my mates will come' etc. which is an important factor in this age group. How can the theatres facilitate independence?

In autumn 1998, under pressure from the deadlines of our own programming, the academic year and the Arts Council, the research to be conducted by Professor Taylor and his colleagues had to begin. We were concerned that the research sample should be representative of the segments outlined above. Aware that the sample in the key areas of Attenders and Gatekeepers would be provided from our box office records, we knew that whether it was representative or not depended on the ability of our marketing materials to influence these target groups to buy tickets.

We aimed for representative diversity, breaking the target group into segments by age, by employment status, and by frequency of theatre attendance. These segments would not necessarily have to be targeted separately, but it was anticipated that data collected from the research exercise would highlight their distinct or shared behaviours or attitudes, together with general trends for future promotion, pricing incentives or programming activity.
[See Section 4].

Tables 1 and 1a show the impact of attempts to fine-tune the sample by employment status between the *pilot phase* and *phase 1* of the project.

Tables 1 and 1a: Sample comparison season by season from questionnaires:

1. *Pilot phase*, autumn 1998:

Occupation	% of audiences
employed	26
student	67
unemployed	1
school/college	3
other	3

1a. *Phase 1*, spring 1999:

Occupation	% of audiences
employed	14
student	64
unemployed	3
school/college	18
other	1

Although the highest proportion remains higher education students, targeting schools appears to have had an impact on the number of school and sixth-form college students who attended. There was also a slight increase in the number of young unemployed attenders. However, the proportion of those at work dropped between autumn '98 and spring '99, despite targeting promotional material at places of work such as the Meadowhall Shopping Centre. The proportion of 22 to 24-year-olds - the age one would most expect to overlap with young workers - is also low in the total sample of both attenders (19%) and non-attenders (17%). Further investigation into reasons for this is required.
[See further research recommendations, Section 4].

21

Section 3 | How Much?
The medium and the message

Examples of fine-tuning activities:

▶ outreach work with schools. From January 1999 onwards, Sheffield Theatres staff visited schools in Sheffield to promote the *How Much?* scheme directly to pupils and to get their feedback.

▶ outreach work with youth groups. In the same period, Sheffield Theatres staff also visited youth groups in the city, with the same purpose. Special effort was made to target areas of the city such as Darnall and Firth Park with a low history of theatre attendance and well-established black and ethnic minority communities. Groups from these communities were given tours of the theatres and explanations of the procedures so that they would feel more comfortable on their first visit to a show. As well as being included in the general marketing, Asian groups were specifically targeted with information about *Goodness Gracious Me.* By the time word-of-mouth on this initiative had spread across Asian youth groups, the event was sold out - leading to some disappointment. However, members of two of the disappointed groups subsequently came to see *Mojo.* [See Attenders, Section 4].

▶ a Sheffield Theatres' young persons' forum pre-existed the *How Much?* project. *How Much?* created a new wave of energy, enabling the forum to meet more regularly, to join discussions with directors and actors, take part in promotions and to give feedback. This group consists of 150 young people aged from 16-24 from a range of backgrounds (working, school, studying, and unemployed).

▶ a specific student forum was set up by Sheffield Theatres through promotions in and around the students' unions at The University of Sheffield, Sheffield Hallam University and Sheffield College. There are currently 45 members of the student forum meeting bi-monthly.

▶ Sheffield Theatres' Crucible youth theatre (160 members) also gave feedback about the *How Much?* scheme.

▶ people at work. A list of workplaces with a high percentage of young people was compiled and targeted with information about special promotions. We also negotiated space for promotion events and offers in 'birthday packs' for young people who work at the Meadowhall shopping centre.

▶ an earlier research project had identified the top ten venues where a cross-section of young people pick up promotional information. These venues, including The Forum, pubs, sports venues, clubs and employment centres, were targeted.

▶ links were made with the Sheffield Hallam University International Society. Joint promotions were carried out during their International Cultural Week to target the Chilean, South East Asian and other international communities in Sheffield.

Programming

Pilot phase: autumn 1998
Introduction
Our programming choices for the *pilot phase* were influenced by three factors. The first two apply in general to any season but the last was specific to the *How Much?* project.

▶ the availability and affordability of performance rights and artistic teams for our own central production (usually a Shakespeare in the autumn season).

▶ the availability and affordability of relevant touring productions (usually more strength in depth in the autumn season).

▶ matching any of the above to one or more of the triggers or 'hot buttons' of the youth market.

Section 1 of this report refers to the fact that the youth market is of commercial interest to many organisations besides theatres. This widespread interest has generated a number of theories and assumptions about young people, especially concerning the triggers or 'hot buttons' that will activate the desired response. In Sheffield Theatres' case, the desired response was twofold:

▶ to buy tickets
▶ to become emotionally involved

Could our programming for the *pilot phase* rise to the challenge of triggering these responses?

Reasons for choosing particular shows to be part of the *How Much?* pilot

Twelfth Night, by William Shakespeare. A Sheffield Theatres production.
- ▶ set GCSE text
- ▶ testing whether the young only come to Shakespeare with school parties or whether they can be tempted to visit the theatre independently
- ▶ directed by one of the UK theatre's rising stars, Michael Grandage

A Clockwork Orange, based on the novel by Anthony Burgess.
- ▶ acclaim and cult status of the book and controversy resulting from the 1972 film's reputation
- ▶ visually stimulating
- ▶ up-to-the minute film and sound techniques
- ▶ 'teenage generation' issues

Popcorn, by Ben Elton.
- ▶ best- selling novel by comedian Ben Elton
- ▶ theme and name recognised by young people
- ▶ production had a national reputation
- ▶ high profile casting (Emma Noble)

Rambert Dance Company, repertoire.
- ▶ encouraging young people to try different art forms
- ▶ testing the level of take-up of dance as opposed to drama
- ▶ containing contemporary music likely to appeal to young people

Outcomes and appraisal

12,000 people aged 16-24 booked for the four productions - a significant increase on the numbers of young people usually attending the theatres. Across previous seasons, the average proportion of young people in the theatre audience was 7%. For the four shows above, 40% were in the 16-24 age group. From box office data, questionnaires and focus groups we learnt that more than 25% were new attenders.

▲ *Illustrations:*
Popcorn *spread from the first* **How Much?** *brochure,* **pilot phase**.
Astor-Tango *spread from* **phase 1** *brochure.*

23

Section 3 | How Much?
The medium and the message

sex...violence...brilliance...shakespeare...all for £3.50*

Questionnaires and focus groups held later revealed that star names, as well as nationally renowned 'cult' products, were of particular appeal to young people and could persuade previous non-attenders to book. The *pilot phase* showed that young people want to be associated with 'risk-taking' products, suggesting that an element of risk-taking in our future programming - along the lines of A Clockwork Orange - would be rewarded by high attendance.

Questionnaire responses, both from current attenders and those who had never been to theatre before, consistently highlighted the strong appeal of modern drama, comedy drama, and stand-up comedy.

Marketing
Pilot phase: autumn 1998
The *pilot phase* was to be launched at Sheffield Hallam University and The University of Sheffield's Freshers' Fayres in October 1998. Prior to the *pilot*, we worked closely with our design agency to develop a *How Much?* house style. We knew that the print-based promotional material had to be distinctive - the students are exposed to literally thousands of pieces of print from different organisations. We also wanted to introduce a strong style and logo that would make an impression and be recognised as the project continued. We wanted the target group, many of whom would be new to Sheffield, to have a sense of the full range of productions available at Sheffield Theatres. We knew we had to emphasise the offer not just in terms of price but also in terms of the other triggers for young people. Without the aid of focus groups, we devised the initial *How Much?* brochure.

The distinctive size and bright colour made the brochure stand out. However, most response was to the tag line on the cover:

'sex...violence...brilliance...shakespeare...all for £3.50'

This appealed not only on price, but also to a sense of risk and difference. Inside the brochure,

▶ we referred to the 'thrills, spills and in your face brilliance of live theatre'
▶ used strong, relevant images

- encouraged people to 'make up your own mind' about
A Clockwork Orange
- emphasised the 'bloodcurdling comedy' of Ben Elton's Popcorn
- highlighted post-show discussions with the cast and backstage
tours on Twelfth Night
- described the dance in terms of its emotional impact
- ran a list of productions of interest to young people 'coming
soon' but not covered by the How Much? scheme's cheap
pricing (e.g. Ardal O'Hanlon, Michael Clark and New Dealers -
a Studio show about the Sheffield Gang Wars)

Between them, we felt these points covered most of the triggers
identified by previous research:

- **Guidance** - sought from sources such as TV and the internet
rather than parents.
- **Heroes** - the influence of idols - from Bart Simpson to Zoe Ball.
- **Identity** - the struggle to assert individual identity.
- **Belonging** - seeking shared experiences, emotions and
reference points.
- **Respect** - seeking respect from peers.
- **Entertainment** - the importance of 'having a good time.'
- **Transparency** - young people are sophisticated consumers
of marketing material. They hate to be patronised. We need
to be honest.

20,000 of the brochures were distributed: around 12,000 hand-to-
hand at Freshers' Fayres and other student events, the remainder
through distribution outlets and direct mail campaigns. The
brochure was added to the list of marketing codes on our box
office system, enabling us to track how many times it came up
as a response to the 'how did you find out about the production?'
query during the sales transaction.

Impact: The brochure generated sales worth £5,700 and was
a prompt for word of mouth on the project in general. However,
focus groups suggested something more pocket-sized for phase 1;
the brochure was too large for leaflet racks

Other marketing activity included:

- adverts were placed in the handbooks Student Pages, Student
Directory and Student Nurse. To help us track their effectiveness
the ads took the form of tear-off vouchers to be handed in at the
box office in order to claim the How Much? discount.

Impact: 63 tear-off vouchers, resulting in sales worth £441,
were returned.

- a promotion was run on the local independent radio station
(Hallam FM) offering the first 60 people to buy a £3.50 ticket
to see Popcorn a free drink and the chance to meet the cast.

Impact: The radio promotion attracted significantly more
bookings than previous radio campaigns, generating 123 sales
(worth £430.50) against an average of three on other shows.
The offer to meet Emma Noble was particularly popular with
young men.

- the Sheffield Theatres website went live in September 1998.
The site was for information rather than on-line sales; however,
it was given a marketing code so that any sales generated
could be tracked. The website address was confirmed too late
to include on all promotional print.

Impact: During the pilot phase, the website attracted 6,952 hits.

Programming
Phase 1: spring 1999
Availability and affordability remained key influences on our
programming decisions. A complicating factor was that the
majority of these decisions had to be taken before the first
wave of research from the pilot phase had been fully analysed.
The programming schedule dictated that the phase 1/spring
1999 season was in place, priced and on sale by November
1998. However, even at this early stage we were aware of
questionnaire and discussion-group feedback - in particular,
the strong appeal of modern drama, comedy drama and
stand-up comedy - which could be tested further in phase 1.

25

Section 3 | How Much?
The medium and the message

In addition, our long-term involvement with the Danceworks contemporary dance programme enabled us to include two dance pieces in this phase. We also responded to the stated willingness of young people to pay more than £3.50 on some productions by setting a slightly higher price (£5) on Sheffield Theatres' central production for the season, Mojo

Reasons for choosing particular shows to be part of *How Much? Phase 1*

Mojo, by Jez Butterworth. A Sheffield Theatres production.

- ▶ one-price house - £5.00
- ▶ modern drama, fast-paced dialogue, ideal for a young audience
- ▶ young actors, attractive all-male cast (starred Alan Westaway, from TV's The Bill)
- ▶ Reservoir Dogs style humour
- ▶ 'sex, drugs and rock'n'roll' theme

Macbeth, by William Shakespeare

- ▶ set GCSE text
- ▶ potential to build on success of Twelfth Night
- ▶ nationally significant production
- ▶ starred TV and film actor Rufus Sewell

Danceworks 99: Random Dance, Shobhana Jeyasingh

- ▶ encouraging young people to try different art forms
- ▶ testing the level of take-up of dance compared with drama
- ▶ Random Dance chosen for its futuristic imagery and use of technology
- ▶ Shobhana Jeyasingh chosen as a contrast to Random Dance and to promote cultural diversity to our young target audiences

Music in the Round: Astor-Tango

- ▶ encouraging young people to try different art forms
- ▶ testing the level of take-up of classical music compared with drama
- ▶ the most accessible piece of the **Music in the Round** season hosted in the Studio Theatre
- ▶ promoting cultural diversity as a perspective-broadening piece

Goodness Gracious Me

- ▶ award-winning BBC television comedy spin-off
- ▶ enabling us to engage in audience development work with young people in the Asian community

Illustration:
Mojo *print image.*

Outcomes and appraisal

7,663 people booked for the six *How Much?* productions.
This was a drop on total sales from the *pilot phase*. Due to
limited availability of *How Much?* tickets on some productions,
the proportion of young people in the audience also dropped from
40% in the *pilot* to 32% in *phase 1*. However, questionnaire and
focus group research indicated that the proportion of new
attenders rose from 25% in the *pilot* to 30% in *phase 1*.

4,619 of the total tickets sold were for Mojo, a production that
was targeted at 16 to 24-year-olds but for which there was no age
bar on the *How Much?* ticket price. In other words, we cannot be
certain that all of the 4,619 attenders fell within the target age
group. If Mojo is removed from the picture, the proportion of
young people in the audience for the other productions remains
higher than not only Sheffield Theatres' pre-*How Much?* figure of
7% but also the TGI figure of 16% that we aimed to match at the
beginning of the project.

Show	% of tickets @ £3.50
Macbeth	33%
Astor-Tango*	4%
Random Dance*	14%
Shobhana Jeyasingh*	5%
Goodness Gracious Me*	30%*
Total Average	**17%**

* for financial reasons, some visiting companies placed limits
  on the number of tickets which could be sold at the *How
  Much?* price.

▲ | *Percentage of total box office
sold at the How Much? price,
excluding Mojo.*

**From the earliest stages, the project was demonstrating
that targeted programming could generate an increase
in young people's attendance.**

As a research exercise, increasing the proportion of attendance
from a previously under-represented group from 7% to 32% in
a matter of months was interesting and rewarding. As a business
exercise, the increase in young people was only valuable if we
could sustain it whilst maintaining our other audiences.

Our experience with Mojo suggested this would be difficult.
Mojo was programmed as Sheffield Theatres' central production
for the spring season. It attracted new audiences, but failed to
attract a sizeable number of our core audience. Informally
collected evidence suggests that in promoting the production
to a youth audience, we were sending a message that excluded
other groups. At this stage, older audiences did not appear
to share our young audience's belief that we should be taking
programming risks. The resulting financial risk would have been
unsustainable without our New Audiences funding.

Mojo had been a critically-acclaimed production which contained
some of the elements young people were telling us would attract
them to the theatre: 'blood and violence', 'well-known [from TV]
actors' etc. The marketing material had contained detailed
information about the plot, as requested by survey respondents
and focus groups ('at the end of the day, you just want to know
what it's about, especially if you've not heard of it'). But the
production hadn't sparked the imaginations of enough younger
(or indeed older) audiences.

For the other productions, particularly the contemporary dance,
the research through surveys and focus groups revealed that
ticket discounts alone would not persuade young people to try
something new. Attenders and non-attenders expressed a caution
about contemporary dance as an 'unknown quantity.' The
dependence on personal recommendations from their peers
was high. [See Section 4].

The impact of academic semesterisation was also felt. Students
now return from the Christmas vacation and are immediately
focused on exams. Our early resolve not to become over-reliant
on the student population was reinforced during this phase.

27

Section 3 | How Much?
The medium and the message

Marketing

Phase 1: spring 1999

Promotional activity for *phase 1* responded to the analysis of the *pilot phase's* impact. In particular, the *pilot phase* brochure was deemed a success in terms of generating sales, and so a second specific *How Much?* brochure was produced. *Phase 1* also saw the *How Much?* press launch and the development of the new Sheffield Theatres' website as a promotional tool.

First, the mundane. With fewer opportunities for hand-to-hand distribution, the brochure was produced to a smaller size so that it would fit in leaflet racks.

Next, the focus groups. They liked orange. They also liked silver. So the brochure was orange and silver. While still attempting to push the 'hot buttons' by appealing to a sense of risk and difference, this second brochure somehow missed the mark - perhaps by being driven by design rather than purpose.

The tag line for *phase 1* was 'murder, mayhem and tango...all for seriously low prices.' The phrase lacked the bite, immediacy and relevance of 'sex...violence...brilliance...shakespeare...all for £3.50' The copy was clearly written but largely obscured by the design. The images available for the chosen productions lacked strength. The focus groups loved it. The marketing team thought it was a mess. 15,000 were produced and distributed through key venues and direct mail to *How Much?* pilot attenders.

Impact: Although 14% of questionnaire respondents cited it as their main source of information, the brochure generated only £401 worth of attributable sales.

Other marketing activity included:

▶ the *How Much?* project public launch, held at The Forum shopping centre on 16 February 1999. The shop unit donated to the project by The Forum had been fitted with floor-to-ceiling images from *How Much?* productions, a sales point was installed and the press invited. At the end of the formalities, a young skateboarder burst through one of the posters, followed by the cast of *Mojo*, who performed a 5-minute section of the play.

Impact: Around 160 young people and project partners attended the launch. The event received coverage on ITV local news, BBC and independent local radio, and in the local and student press. At the sales point, however, the take-up was negligible.

▶ specific direct mail campaigns were triggered on all the *How Much?* productions. These campaigns targeted previous attenders from the *pilot phase* - the same group for whom a brochure mailing had not been a purchasing trigger.

Impact: Direct mail campaigns generated sales worth £37,269

▶ in an effort to encourage crossover between Sheffield's vibrant clubbing scene and the theatres, joint promotions were run with the nearby Leadmill nightclub for two shows in the season - one with *How Much?* pricing (Mojo), and one at full-price (Boogie Nights). Two nights were chosen and promoted as 'see the show, then party with the cast.' A ticket for either show doubled as a drinks' token at the club.

Impact: 80 young people took advantage of the promotion

▶ for *phase 1*, the Sheffield Theatres website address was included on all *How Much?* printed material.

Impact: The website attracted 17,113 hits, an increase of 146% on the *pilot phase*.

Programming

Phase 2a and 2b - summer and autumn 1999

Programming the latter stages of the project - *phases 2a and 2b* - presented the first real opportunity to step off the treadmill, incorporate some of the learning from the research so far and address artistic development issues. The period covered (April to November 1999) contained three of our own productions - Angels in America, A View from the Bridge and 23:59 - as well as toured-in work. Angels and 23:59 were specifically targeted at the *How Much?* audience.

Research showed that the Crucible auditorium was proving popular with young attenders because of its informality and 'closer, more intimate' atmosphere. The non-attenders research was also revealing attitudes towards the theatre ('stuffy', 'for older people', 'somewhere you go with your school/mum and dad') which the physical experience of the Crucible could counteract - if we could get them through the doors.

New Audiences funding enabled the theatres to commission a new play to be developed with and for young people for performance in autumn 1999. [The process of commissioning and developing this play is described in Section 5]. New Audiences funding also enabled us to programme a summer production in the Crucible for the first time in several years.

Since the *pilot phase*, our young attenders had been encouraging us to take programming risks. The non-attenders were suggesting that 'spectacle' would encourage them to attend. Having focused primarily on increasing the volume of attendance by young people, we were anxious to commit more time to developing the quality of our engagement with particular excluded groups. This feedback combined with our wish to make a strong artistic statement and resulted in us programming Tony Kushner's Angels in America Part One: Towards the Millennium.

In addition to the three factors which underpin all programming decisions outlined on page 21, our programming for *phases 2a and 2b* was influenced by two further considerations:

▶ the analysis of attender and non-attender questionnaire and focus group feedback

▶ our desire to develop qualitative relationships with particular market segments.

Illustrations:
- *The* **'Murder, mayhem...'** *brochure from* **Phase 1** *(Cover).*
- *Robot flyer.*

29

Section 3 | How Much?
The medium and the message

Reasons for choosing particular shows to be part of *How Much? phases 2a* and *2b*

2a

Angels in America Part One: Towards the Millennium, by Tony Kushner.
A Sheffield Theatres production.

▶ modern drama with comic elements - category highly rated both by attenders and non-attenders
▶ cultural diversity - gay themes
▶ artistic validation - a new production and a new direction for the theatres
▶ play designed with young audience in mind
▶ spectacular, large-scale stage design
▶ opportunities for developing links with gay youth groups and agencies

Danceworks 99: Nederlands Dans Theater 2 **(repertoire)**,
Siobhan Davies (Wild Air), Darshan Singh Bhuller (Planted Seeds)

▶ encouraging young people to try different art forms
▶ testing the level of take-up of dance compared with drama
▶ cultural diversity (one dealing with the political and religious struggles in Sarajevo)

The Winter's Tale, by William Shakespeare. Performed by the Maly Drama Theatre of St Petersburg

▶ award-winning production - world famous company
▶ artistic validation
▶ associated training workshops for youth theatre members
▶ challenging, foreign-language production
▶ opportunities for developing links with different educational organisations

Music Theatre London: Die Fledermaus/Eugene Onegin

▶ education packages that come with Music Theatre London - 'feel as though you're participating'
▶ different art form - broadening the scope of performances which young people attend
▶ two accessible classics
▶ spectacle

2b

One Flew Over the Cuckoo's Nest, based on the novel
by Ken Kesey

▶ modern drama with comic elements - category highly rated
both by attenders and non-attenders

▶ reputation of the film

▶ well-known cast (from TV appearances)

▶ opportunities to develop links with mental health care agencies

A View from the Bridge, by Arthur Miller. A Sheffield Theatres
production.

▶ modern drama - highly-rated category, particularly with non-
attenders in the 22-24 age group

▶ schools' and university set text

▶ opportunities to strengthen links with The University of
Sheffield drama department

The Colour of Justice, based on the McPherson report into the
death of Stephen Lawrence

▶ dramatisation of actual events

▶ pertinent issues - meets positive educational aspirations of
attenders and non-attenders

▶ cultural diversity - 'learn to understand experiences alien to our
own lives'

▶ opportunities to develop links with black communities and anti-
racist agencies

23:59, by Nicola Baldwin. A Sheffield Theatres production

▶ one price house - £4.50

▶ show about youth and music with a Sheffield perspective

▶ written for, and in consultation with teams of young people
aged 16-24, living in Sheffield

Outcomes and appraisal

12,968 young people booked for the 10 productions covered
by phases 2a and 2b, meaning that the proportion of 16 to
24-year-olds in the total audience for these productions was 42%.
New attenders dropped to 22% in phase 2a, but rose to 36% in
phase 2b - the highest proportion of new attenders for any phase
of the project.

The risk-taking element of the programme had mixed effect:

▶ unlike Mojo, Angels in America attracted not only a sizeable
proportion of young people (35%) in the total audience,
but was also rewarded by the return of our core drama
audience - becoming the 'hot ticket' production in the region
for summer 1999.

▶ 23:59, the new work commissioned from Nicola Baldwin, was
badly received by local and national press critics. However, it
attracted an average of 92 young people per performance - a
very respectable audience for new writing - and has since been
nominated for an international award. [See Section 5].

Marketing

Phases 2a and 2b - summer and autumn 1999
The promotion of phases 2a and 2b remained heavily print-based
but also contained strategies for responding to the mid-term
research findings. Surveys and focus groups reflected what we
knew about the 16 to 24-year-olds from our box office records:

▶ that word of mouth was particularly important

▶ that they responded more to posters than other age groups.

However, the research was able to break this down further. So we
started to see differences between, for example, the triggers for
16 to 18-year-olds and those for 22 to 24-year-olds.

Our fingers had been burnt by producing the phase 1 brochure
to a brief from focus groups. Nonetheless, we continued to consult
focus groups on print design. The 150 young people who discussed
the print for phases 2a and 2b concluded that the phase 1 How
Much? brochure was too fussy and too difficult to read.

31

Section 3 | How Much?
The medium and the message

The focus groups also felt that young people were beginning to relate to the *How Much?* logo and the use of orange and silver print. They liked the idea of a pocket-sized brochure, something that could be stuck on a wall and/or 'unusual shapes'. We also wanted to test some contradictory feedback about the amount of information the print should carry. Some young people wanted as much detail of the plot and cast as possible. Others claimed that they found too much information off-putting and that a tag line was all that was necessary. As a result, two new pieces of print were produced: 10,000 silver *How Much?* brochures and 10,000 'robot' flyers.

The brochure gave a synopsis of each production; the robot carried only basic information. The print was distributed to the young person's distribution list as updated during *phase 1*, posted to previous *How Much?* bookers, and included in the mailshots of venues such as The Showroom cinema and The Leadmill.

Impact: The effectiveness of the *How Much?* brochure increased throughout the project, from 14% in *phase 1* through to 15% and 17% in *phases 2a* and *2b* respectively. Measured against the impact of the robot flyer, the brochure was 69% more successful in generating ticket sales.

Other marketing activity included:

Work to engage with different social and educational groups took two forms:

- ▶ direct mail and telesales inviting the groups to participate in pre-arranged workshops
- ▶ working with gatekeepers and group members to develop workshops and other ancillary activities

The former aimed to increase the range of our contacts with relevant groups. We recognised that our database was limited and, being based on box office records, it was composed chiefly of previous attenders. We purchased two mailing lists to beef up our database:

- ▶ sixth-formers in South Yorkshire with an interest in the arts
- ▶ 5,000 young listeners to contemporary music (from the Britannia Music Club)

Impact: The average response to direct mail in the *pilot phase* and *phase 1* of the project was 31% and 32% respectively. The response rate rose to 38% across *phases 2a* and *2b*.

Angels in America and *The Colour of Justice* provided specific opportunities for development work with communities who are under-represented in Sheffield Theatres' core audience.

- ▶ *Angels in America*. The links that already existed with gay clubs in the city were extended to cover in-depth work with various social and issue-based groups. For example, we involved the Centre for HIV and Sexual Health at the earliest stage. The Centre met with the play's director, ran workshops for gay young men, contributed an article to the production's programme, brought groups to see the play and had an information stall in the theatre foyer.
- ▶ *The Colour of Justice*. As well as working with different schools and community groups such as Sheffield and District Afro-Caribbean Community Association (SADACCA) to encourage attendance, the theatres hosted three debates on the issues raised by the production. Senior police officers, the chief executive of Sheffield City Council, the director of SADACCA and a representative from the Commission for Racial Equality took part in question and answer sessions with members of the audience. A direct phone link to South Yorkshire's Chief Constable was also set up in the theatre foyer.

Impact: The views expressed at the debates and on the phone link are forming part of an ongoing consultation process between the police and Sheffield's black and ethnic minority communities.

Conclusion

In all, 21 productions were programmed under the *How Much?* banner. They attracted more than 32,000 ticket sales to young people in the period between September 1998 and November 1999. Including the *pilot phase*, young people constituted an average of 41% - with new young attenders averaging 28% - of the total audience for those 21 productions.

The numbers are a measurable impact of Sheffield Theatres' activities. But *How Much?* was concerned not only with the quantity of young people attending Sheffield Theatres. We gave equal weight to the quality of our engagement with young people.

Revisiting the modified objectives outlined on page 18, the experience of programming and promoting the *How Much?* project has clearly had an impact. Some of our ideas have been confirmed, some have changed and our perspective has been broadened in some key areas.

To explore the importance of programming, ticket price and promotion as a practical issue in access to theatre performances for the broad population - and especially for the young (16-24).

The research findings in Section 4 explore the impact of pricing in more detail, but the activities outlined in this section lend additional insight to the issue of programming and promotion. The *How Much?* project was never intended to produce a definitive checklist for successful promotion to 16 to 24-year-olds - much less a checklist for artistic decision-making. However, it has taught us some important lessons about getting the balance right between consulting the audience and using our professional judgement. For example,

► we produced one piece of print (the *phase 1* brochure) in response to focus group suggestions and against our better judgement. Losing sight of the purpose of marketing communications (to impart information and generate sales) could have been an expensive mistake.

► although Mojo was an excellent production, there were elements its selection: modern drama, risk-taking plot, cinematic violence, young male cast, etc. which were perhaps transmitted to our audiences as 'checklist programming'. Angels in America (potentially a much more 'risky' artistic endeavour) communicated passion, excitement and spectacle in a more transparent way. In doing so, it appealed both to young and older audiences.

33

Section 3 | How Much?
The medium and the message |

To find realistic ways in which theatre can use ticket pricing, programming and promotion to encourage greater cultural diversity amongst its audiences.

The *How Much?* activities served to confirm one rather obvious point, and to broaden our perspective on how cultural diversity might be achieved.

Attenders and non-attenders agree that for a production to appeal to them, it has to have some relevance to their lives and interests. This does not have to be taken literally in the sense of, for example, 'young Asian women will only go to productions about young Asian women'. But it confirms the centrality of relevant programming. For example,

▶ in retrospect, the overall strength of the *How Much?* productions in the *pilot* season was not matched by any of the subsequent phases - hence the exceptionally high levels of attendance in autumn 1998. However, in *phases 1*, *2a* and *2b* we were able not only to maintain audience numbers but also to programme productions like Goodness Gracious Me, Shobana Jeyasingh, Angels in America and The Colour of Justice, where the potential for audience development was more focused on culturally diverse groups.

To develop working partnerships with arts, community and other groups in order to enhance access.

In addressing partnerships, we also increase the potential for sustainability:

To investigate ways to ensure the longer-term sustainability of the project.

Partnerships forged through the *How Much?* project have continued beyond the term of our New Audiences funding. Professional organisations, community groups, gatekeepers and artists first approached as part of the project continue to play an active part in audience development work. Importantly, the project has enabled Sheffield Theatres to reassert its position as a resource for these groups and individuals. We believe the continued development of these partnerships is essential not only for developing new audiences but also for attracting sustained funding support for the project. For example,

▶ developing workshops with the Centre for HIV and Sexual Health during the run of Angels in America will influence training initiatives for young workers (an under-represented group in the original sample) run in conjunction with potential partners such as the Benefits Agency, the Employment Service and Sheffield Young Carers' Project.

▶ the strategic decision to programme work by Asian artists as part of *How Much?* has led to our becoming a partner in a South Asian audience and artistic development project ('Arts Exchange') run through West Yorkshire Arts Marketing. Arts Exchange has enabled staff from all departments in the theatre to attend awareness-raising training sessions. It will culminate in an exhibition of work by young people from the Asian community in January 2001 and the performance of a specially commissioned professional piece later that year.

Summary of How Much? | ▶
productions, showing number of
tickets sold at How Much? prices,
and percentage of young people
aged 16-24 in the total audience. |

Pilot - autumn 1998	Dates	Performances	Venue	How Much? tickets sold	% young people in audience
A Clockwork Orange	20-24/10/9	6	Crucible	2,721	56
Popcorn	26-31/10/98	8	Lyceum	3,946	47
Twelfth Night	12/11-5/12/98	22	Crucible	5,027	44
Rambert Dance	25-28/11/98	5	Lyceum	376	13
			Total	12,070	40

Phase 1 - spring '99	Dates	Performances	Venue	How Much? Tickets sold	% young people in audience
Mojo	11/02-6/03/99	19	Crucible	4,619	100*
Macbeth	15-20/02/99	8	Lyceum	2,659	33
Goodness Gracious Me	22/02/99	1	Lyceum	325	30
Astor-Tango	04/03/99	1	Studio	17	5
Random Dance	24/03/99	1	Crucible	23	14
Shobana Jeyasingh	26/03/99	1	Crucible	20	9
			Total	7,663	32

Phase 2a - summer '99	Dates	Performances	Venue	How Much? Tickets sold	% young people in audience
Nederlands Dans Theater 2	17-18/05/99	2	Lyceum	290	59
The Winter's Tale	19-22/05/99	4	Crucible	254	21
Eugene Onegin/Die Fledermaus	20-22/05/99	3	Lyceum	91	10
Planted Seeds	26/05/99	1	Lyceum	42	21
Wild Air	28-29/05/99	2	Lyceum	78	23
Angels in America	04-19/06/99	14	Crucible	1,096	35
			Total	1,851	28

Phase 2b - autumn '99	Dates	Performances	Venue	How Much? Tickets sold	% young people in audience
A View from the Bridge	23/09-16/10/99	23	Crucible	4,984	55
The Colour of Justice	19-23/10/99	7	Crucible	1,591	50
One Flew Over the Cuckoo's Nest	01-06/11/99	8	Lyceum	2,886	48
23:59	05-27/11/99	18	Crucible	1,656	100*
			Total	11,117	63
			PROJECT TOTALS	32,701	41

*estimate

Section 4

Research

Background and introduction
Attenders
Non-attenders
Gatekeepers

Paul Moriarty in **A View from the Bridge** *written by Arthur Miller*

Finding the right questions

It is no secret that the issue of young people's attendance of and participation in the arts is complex and diverse. In the 'pre-pilot' phase of *How Much?* Sheffield Theatres tried to make this a more manageable question, developing our ideas to a point where they became deliverable and researchable.

Our question, simply put, is:

'How does the mix of programming, price and promotion influence young people's attendance of Sheffield Theatres?'

We were conscious that this question is far from simple, containing as it does, three variables, programming, price, and promotion.

However, it is a real world question, reflecting an environment where these variables exist and are manipulated on a daily basis. Doing this is our business. We routinely identify areas for potential market growth or market penetration. We programme productions that have an appeal to these target markets. We promote the product. Crucially, the *How Much?* funding gave us more leeway to set ticket prices at levels that we thought these markets could bear.

Research methods

The basic methodological approach focused on the three key variables, their measurement, analysis and manipulation. We used our existing methods of data collection (see below) with additional methods for specific aspects of the project. Finding out how many young people attend, how often, how much they pay etc. was dealt with through box office data collection, with the addition of questionnaires and surveys. Box office records provided initial numerical data concerning gender, postcode, frequency of attendance etc. Questionnaires were used to collect information on other expenditure, area of residence, patterns of social life and so on. Beyond the quantitative, there is always the qualitative. In-depth interviews and focus groups were used to find out more about when, why and how young people will attend theatre. Focus groups also provided a base for more complex exploration of the constraints, including perceptual constraints, to theatre attendance that emerged from the surveys. We also undertook qualitative analysis of promotional material and the theatre environment.

Finding the samples

The *How Much?* project was aimed initially at 16 to 24-year-olds. We employed standard measures for the key variables of class and gender as one means of gaining representative cross-sections. The research also 'drilled down' to variables that better reflect the complexities of modern life: different stages of maturity within the age band; employment status; education status, etc. We were aiming for and achieved a sample size of around 1,000 to enable meaningful cross-tabulation. The potential sample was increased by distribution of targeted material to undergraduate and further education students. Although students form a key constituency for Sheffield Theatres, we were conscious that not all young people are students. We also developed links with employers to access young workers, and with training agencies to reach the young unemployed. The sample identified young people with a mix of interest in different types of arts/entertainment, and divided these into three categories of 'theatregoer':

▶ non-attenders
▶ infrequent attenders
▶ frequent attenders

Pilot phase

Given our aim that the research be as explicit, precise and systematic as possible, it was vital that we conduct a *pilot phase* to test the questionnaire design and the other research tools. The research data for this phase was collected using the following methods:

▶ Sheffield Theatres' box office system (BOCS) collects name and address records (NARs) together with basic marketing information, including purchasing 'triggers'. The system is part of a network with other city venues and can track attendance across other venues/artforms.

▶ postcodes with the highest density of students and young people were identified through available area profiles.

▶ post-performance questionnaires were used to assess triggers, response to performance etc. and test triggers/barriers to future attendance.

Questionnaires were piloted on autumn '98 productions to ensure they were 'do-able' and to monitor the effectiveness of different ways of handing them out - direct, left on seats, pre, mid or post performance etc.

At the autumn '98 stage, we were also negotiating a deal with a telecoms company that would enable us to collect specific quantitative information from respondents through telephone questionnaires. Unfortunately, this did not materialise. As negotiations progressed, it became clear that while the company would welcome the promotional opportunities, servicing the potential volume of business would be costly to them and might also overstretch their technical resources.

In the *pilot phase*, take-up of *How Much?* tickets was tracked through discount and marketing codes and NARs on the box office system. The impact of targeted marketing communications, including the new website, was tracked through the box office system and there was a trial run of questionnaires. These methods continued to be used as the project developed.

Questionnaires and surveys were administered and analysed by the research team from The University of Sheffield and Sheffield Hallam University. The team also set up focus groups to collect, analyse and identify trends in qualitative data. These focus groups, together with the theatres' students' and young people's forums discussed the relevance/appeal of programming and marketing communications in particular.

It is also worth noting that we planned but failed to conduct the following analysis (due to time constraints):

▶ tracking and cross-referencing postcode penetration against potential;
▶ a literature review of other research projects to identify similarities and/or local variance.

Research concerning awareness of, responses to and interest in the *How Much?* project

Authors:

Peter Taylor, professor of leisure management, Management School, The University of Sheffield

Sophie Withnall, research assistant, School of Leisure and Food Management, Sheffield Hallam University

Elizabeth Owen, senior lecturer, School of Leisure and Food Management, Sheffield Hallam University

Introduction

The following sections report the findings of the research conducted by staff and students at Sheffield Hallam University and The University of Sheffield in conjunction with Sheffield Theatres in the main phases of the *How Much?* project:

▶ *phase 1* spring 1999
▶ *phase 2a* summer 1999
▶ *phase 2b* autumn 1999

(This section does not cover preliminary research conducted in the *pilot phase* of the project in autumn 1998).

The aim of the research was to establish awareness of, attitudes to, interest in and responses to the project by three groups of people:

▶ young attenders;
▶ young non-attenders;
▶ 'gatekeepers' (key people who act as informal agents for Sheffield Theatres in informing young people of productions and possibly accompanying them to performances).

The research was designed to inform the *How Much?* project and any subsequent policy developed to attract young people to Sheffield Theatres. Academic staff and volunteer student researchers from both Sheffield universities used four different research methods:

1. **an audience survey of young people attending Sheffield Theatres, throughout the spring, summer and autumn 1999 phases of *How Much?***
2. **focus groups with both regular and first-time theatre attenders, in the spring and summer 1999 phases of the project**
3. **a survey of student non-attenders, in spring 1999**
4. **interviews with gatekeepers for young potential attenders, in spring 1999.**

The first section reports on the results of the young attender audience survey and focus groups. The second section analyses the findings from the survey of non-attenders. The third section examines the views of gatekeepers. A final section identifies other research needs of relevance to any continuing policy, post *How Much?*

RESULTS AND ANALYSIS OF *HOW MUCH?* YOUNG ATTENDERS RESEARCH

1.1 Introduction

Self-completion questionnaires were returned by 1000 16 to 24-year-olds attending a total of 21 Sheffield Theatres' productions between February and November 1999. Seventeen of the productions were priced at a reduced *How Much?* price (fifteen at £3.50, one at £5.00 and one at £4.50), and four were standard price productions. Details of this are provided in Table 1.1. Student volunteers from both Sheffield universities distributed the attender questionnaires as respondents entered the theatre. The volunteers asked if the respondent was in the age group 16-24 years before distributing the questionnaire and briefing the respondent on the purpose and the protocol for completing it. Respondents self-completed the questionnaires and handed them in to volunteers at the end of the performance (alternatively there was a box for late returns after the performance, whilst a few respondents posted their completed questionnaires). The attenders' questionnaire sought to investigate the following topics:

▶ socio-demographic characteristics
▶ previous theatre attendance
▶ response to publicity and promotional materials
▶ response to ticket prices
▶ expenditure on leisure
▶ response to the experience of attending Sheffield Theatres.

▼ | *Table 1.1 - productions surveyed and returns received*

Production	Type of Production	Returned Questionnaires	Number of tickets sold at *How Much?* price
Mojo	contemporary drama	123	4619 (all at £5.00)
Macbeth	classical drama	68	2659
Goodness Gracious Me	popular show	29	325
Astor-Tango	classical music	6	17
Sulphur 16	dance	29 **	23
Shobana Jeyasingh	dance	17	20
The Rocky Horror Show*	popular show	30	0
NDT2	dance	73	290
The Winter's Tale	classical drama	52	254
Eugene Onegin	opera	19	26
Die Fledermaus	opera	12	65
Planted Seeds	dance	26	42
Wild Air	dance	17	78
Angels in America	contemporary drama	100	1096
Happy Days*	popular show	15	0
The Things We Do for Love*	contemporary drama	6	0
After Juliet*	contemporary drama	4	0
A View from the Bridge	modern classic	86	4984
The Colour of Justice	contemporary drama	125	1591
One Flew Over the Cuckoo's Nest	contemporary drama	137	2886
23:59	contemporary drama	26	1656
TOTAL		**1,000**	**20,631**

* Denotes a non *How Much?* production.
** The higher number of returned questionnaires than *How Much?* tickets sold is a result of complimentary tickets being distributed.

1.2 Focus groups

A total of nine focus groups were conducted during the *How Much?* project. Three took place with students at Sheffield Hallam University who had never visited Sheffield Theatres before. They were given tickets to see a performance of Mojo and their responses to their first visits to Sheffield Theatres and the *How Much?* project were explored.

Three further focus groups took place with students from Sheffield Hallam University attending their first contemporary dance production. These groups investigated their responses to the performance, the venue and publicity material for dance.

Three groups took place approximately half way through the project, in the late spring/early summer of 1999, with young regular theatre attenders who had been to see more than one production at Sheffield Theatres in the *How Much?* programme. The discussions focused around: opinions of past productions seen at Sheffield Theatres, views on price, the extent of awareness of *How Much?* responses to print, to the theatre and possible incentives to encourage young people to attend.

1.3 People

1.3.1 Attender survey respondents' characteristics

Age	%
<16 years	2
16 -18 years	30
19 -21 years	47
22 -24 years	19
>24 years	2

Gender	%
Female	73
Male	27

Occupation	%
Employed	14
Unemployed	3
Training scheme	1
School	18
FE College	10
University	54

Type of performance	%
Contemporary drama	61
Classical drama	12
Dance, opera, classical music	20
Popular shows	7

How Much? show	%
Yes	94
No	6

Theatre	%
Crucible	53
Lyceum	46
Studio	1

▲ | *Table 1.2 - attender survey characteristics*

The highest number of survey responses was received from females, aged 19-21 who were university students. This profile of respondents echoes Target Group Index (TGI) data, the only major national survey to regularly question people about arts participation. TGI shows a high percentage of females in socio economic group AB attending the theatre most regularly. The majority of productions surveyed were *How Much?* shows, contemporary drama and took place in the Crucible Theatre.

1.3.2   New audiences

The percentages of first-time attenders to Sheffield Theatres varied throughout all three phases in 1999 *(phase 1* spring, *phase 2a* summer, *phase 2b* autumn), decreasing in the summer phase and increasing greatly in the autumn. A possible explanation for this could be students leaving Sheffield during the summer *(phase 2a)* and returning during the autumn *(phase 2b)*.

Visit	Phase 1 Spring '99 %	Phase 2a Summer '99 %	Phase 2b Autumn '99 %	All phases %
First visit	30	22	36	29
1 - 3 shows	41	40	36	39
4 - 6 shows	21	25	20	22
>7 shows	8	14	9	10

▲ | *Table 1.3 - frequency of visits to Sheffield Theatres in the last twelve months*

The responses received from first-time attenders both from the questionnaires and from the focus groups were largely positive. Of all the first-time attenders from the survey data, 93% stated they felt encouraged return to Sheffield Theatres. One questionnaire respondent commented,

"Before moving to Sheffield, I had never been (to the theatre)...thanks for introducing me".

1.3.3 Previous attenders

The survey data shows that the young people attending Sheffield Theatres are not in the main a new audience. There are indications from the focus groups and qualitative comments on questionnaires that *How Much?* has been successful in encouraging young people who already attend the theatre to both visit on a more regular basis and attend a broader range of productions. This view is exemplified by one questionnaire respondent, who stated,

"By taking advantage of the How Much? *offers, I have seen some productions I would not have considered before".*

1.4 Programming

1.4.1 Programme in relation to new audiences

The shows which attracted the largest proportions of first-time attenders were Mojo (36%), Macbeth (31%), Goodness Gracious Me (40%), The Rocky Horror Show (37%), Die Fledermaus (33%), Wild Air (41%), A View from the Bridge (38%) and The Colour of Justice (44%). There was no evident pattern in the productions which young people chose to see when they attended Sheffield Theatres for the first time.

A female in the attenders' focus group reported that many of her Asian friends had visited the theatre for the first time to see Goodness Gracious Me. She felt that by putting on a production predominately for an Asian audience, the theatres had made themselves accessible for young Asian people. She stated:

"I remember bringing someone who hadn't been to the theatres before and she was really taken aback, like wow, wow...and she knew the play. I think what was in her mind was like theatre's more for formal people, with money and not for Asian women like herself; very much white based".

1.5   Promotion

1.5.1   Communication

Word of mouth was the largest source of information to which people had responded and was cited by 40% of survey respondents, as shown in Table 1.4. Word of mouth was particularly important for those people attending dance, opera or classical music (42%), university students (50%), people who had seen 1-3 shows at Sheffield Theatres in the last year (43%), and 19-21 year olds (44%). Young people's reliance on recommendations from other people was conveyed strongly in focus groups (both with attenders and non-attenders). By using this means of communication, participants felt that they were minimising any risk.

The effectiveness of the *How Much?* brochure as a means of communication increased throughout the project: *phase 1* 14%, *phase 2a* 15% and *phase 2b* 17%. Similarly, the use of word of mouth increased from 30% in *phase 1* to 45% in *phase 2b*, suggesting that knowledge of the project had spread over time.

1.5.2   Print

The second highest source of information cited was the specific *How Much?* brochure (16%). Frequent attenders at minority art forms - dance, opera and classical music - had the highest response to the more specialised *How Much?* brochures.

This was reinforced in the focus group with attenders in which it was stated,

"I actually look for stuff so that's how I know what's going on".

▼ | Table 1.4
  | - information sources

Source	Total % of respondents	DOC %	Classical Autumn '99 %	Contemporary drama %	Popular Shows %
Word of mouth	40	42	33	39	40
How Much? brochure	16	18	16	16	4
Season brochure in the post	12	11	18	10	20
Season brochure picked up	7	9	8	7	4
Flyer in the post	7	6	3	8	9
Flyer picked up	7	10	5	6	10
Poster	6	2	4	8	3
Newspaper	4	0	0	10	4
Other	4	2	1	7	4
Radio	3	0	0	0	3

Note - DOC is an abbreviation for dance, opera and classical music

The percentage of first-time visitors who found out about the production through print is lower than for more frequent attenders. One first-time attender stated,

"I don't think I ever really look for things like that".

Indeed, the percentage who cited the *How Much?* brochures as their source of information increases with the frequency of visits: 10% for first-time attenders and 26% for those who had seen over seven shows at Sheffield Theatres in the last twelve months. Conversely, picking up a standard theatre season brochure was more likely to be done by first-time attenders (9%) than those who had seen more than seven shows (6%). First-time attenders were much more likely to respond to word of mouth (49%) than any other group. These findings indicate that special promotional *How Much?* print was most effective for those people who had already visited the theatre.

1.5.3   Content of print

First-time attenders emphasised that print needed to be clear; focus group participants commented:

"If it's eye-catching and you don't understand, you'd probably throw it away".

They felt that print needed to convey as much information as possible. It was felt that a clear outline of exactly what the product was, would be the largest selling point, particularly for new productions,

"at the end of the day you just want to know what it's about, especially if you've not heard of it".

Participants wanted to know what type of show it would be,

"I'd like to know if it's a comedy or a tragedy, so you'll know whether you'll be laughing or crying".

an outline of the production, and a recommendation from a trusted source,

"I'd want something else, like what the press had said, so it's not so anonymous".

1.5.4   Incentives to visit the theatre

The most popular incentives which respondents felt would attract them to visit the theatre were: a young person's discount (86%), a free drink with a ticket (69%) and deals with bars and clubs (47%), as shown in Table 1.5. The popularity of non price-related incentives perhaps indicates a desire for a greater social aspect to visiting the theatre.

Promotion	All respondents	16 - 18 years	19 - 21 years	22 - 24 years
Young person's discount	86	84	88	87
Free drink with ticket	69	78	65	66
Deals with bars/clubs	47	62	43	29
Late night bars	42	52	39	36
Deals with public transport	41	49	40	33
Meet the cast	36	46	31	32
Young person's night	35	47	31	28
Live music in the bar/foyer	30	39	26	27
Pre/post performance workshops	24	30	21	18

▲ *Table 1.5 - respondents by age 'very interested' in incentives*

It is interesting to note that a higher percentage of respondents (48%) in the 16-18 years category were very interested in a young person's night. This indicates that for marketing purposes, the label 'young person' appeals more to the people at the lower end of the 16-24 category. All incentives show a decline in enthusiasm as the respondent's age increases, except for the idea of a discount on ticket prices.

More frequent attenders were more attracted by incentives than new attenders. For the latter, it appears that it is the production that has the greatest influence.

1.6   Price

1.6.1   Financial constraints

Financial constraints were cited most frequently as deterring young people from visiting the theatre more often, [as Table 1.6 shows] with, 'Don't have enough money', the most frequently cited of all the constraints prompted.

It is perhaps significant that the perception of the theatres as expensive decreases throughout the 12 months of the *How Much?* project covered by the research. The likely explanation for this is that awareness of the reduced ticket prices increased over time, thereby spreading the perception that the theatres are reasonably priced, not expensive.

1.6.2   Value for money

The majority of respondents to the survey felt the value for money they had received was excellent (57%) or good (32%). This data is substantiated by focus group discussions in which participants felt the *How Much?* ticket prices were good value. One participant stated,

"I wouldn't argue with paying £3.50 for a night's entertainment".

Another person from the same group compared the *How Much?* prices with the price of going to the cinema,

"The cinema is so much more expensive and this is only £3.50 - you get much more out of this".

Discussions in focus groups and qualitative comments on questionnaires show that if young people are going to try something new, they wish to ensure they will receive value for money. Paying a high price for theatre tickets is perceived as high risk. One questionnaire respondent wrote,

"The How Much? *scheme is excellent, as it is not a waste of money if you don't enjoy the production".*

Constraint	All phases %	Phase 1 Spring %	Phase 2a Summer %	Phase 2b Autumn %
Ticket prices too high	46	52	52	37
Don't have enough money	62	61	64	60
Theatres are expensive	26	31	27	21
Theatres are reasonably priced	47	45	44	51

▲ | *Table 1.6 - responses to questions relating to monetary constraints*

Performance	Prepared to pay more? %
Mojo	43
Macbeth	55
Goodness Gracious Me	55
Astor-Tango	80
Sulphur 16	40
Shobana Jeyasingh	67
The Rocky Horror Show*	48
NDT2	82
The Winter's Tale	72
Eugene Onegin	33
Die Fledermaus	33
Planted Seeds	58
Wild Air	44
Angels in America	71
Happy Days*	71
The Things We Do for Love*	0
After Juliet	0
A View from the Bridge	65
The Colour of Justice	59
One Flew Over the Cuckoo's Nest	56
23:59	35

*Denotes a non *How Much?* production

▲ | *Table 1.7 - prepared to pay more by performance*

1.6.3 Will people pay more?

Of the survey respondents, 58% stated that they would have been prepared to pay more for their ticket. The extra amounts they were prepared to pay ranged from 50 pence to over £3.00, with 46% prepared to pay a further £2.50 or more.

For 14 out of the 21 shows surveyed a higher proportion of respondents were willing to pay more than those who were not, as shown in Table 1.7. It should be noted that for Happy Days which was not a *How Much?* performance, 70% of respondents were prepared to pay more, endorsing the notion that it is the programme rather than the price that attracts young people.

Focus group discussions revealed that young people were more likely to pay more for a show that was well-known, because they felt they had a guarantee of enjoyment. In response to the question, 'would you pay £10 to see a show?' one participant stated,

"If it's something I know I'll enjoy".

1.6.4 Leisure expenditure

The following table shows the respondents' average weekly spending on going out:

Weekly leisure spend on 'nights out'	%
< £20	32
£20 < £45	24
£45 < £70	31
£70 < £100	8
£100+	6

▲ | *Table 1.8 - weekly spending on nights out*

These figures show that young people spend a considerable amount of money on leisure, but the high number of people who cited 'Don't have enough money' as a constraint to attending the theatre suggests that they choose not to spend it on going to the theatre. This suggests that price is not a major deterrent if the show is right. One focus group participant believed that going to the theatre was simply not a leisure activity for young people;

"It's a generation thing isn't it? As you get older, you slow down so you're more likely to sit and watch a performance passively rather than go to pubs and clubs".

1.7 Place

1.7.1 Responses to the experience of attending Sheffield Theatres

Responses to visiting Sheffield Theatres were largely positive. From the questionnaire sample, 94% felt encouraged to visit again. The adjectives most often used to describe Sheffield Theatres were thought-provoking (54%) and exciting (50%).

Responses from first-time attenders to visiting Sheffield Theatres were varied. The common initial response to the Crucible was that it was smaller than people had expected. First-time attenders commented on the informality of the Crucible,

"It's not like a proper night out, where everyone gets dressed up".

Several focus groups also stated that they associated the Crucible with more contemporary productions;

"If it's a modern play, I expect it to be in the Crucible, 'cos it's closer, more intimate".

1.8 Conclusions

The research on young people attending Sheffield Theatres for the *How Much?* project has shown that a considerable number of first-time attenders visited Sheffield Theatres during the project. Young people's responses to their first visit to Sheffield Theatres were extremely positive and most felt that they would return.

The *How Much?* audience, aged 16-24, primarily consists of female, university students who are aged between 19-21 years old. The research showed some significant differences between different age categories within the 16-24 years group. It is important to remember therefore that this group is not homogeneous in its opinions and motivations.

The majority of young people surveyed perceived £3.50 to be good value for money for a theatre ticket, but felt that if the production was well-known they would be ready to pay more.

Young people rely primarily upon word of mouth as a means of finding out the programme at Sheffield Theatres. They felt this reduced the risk involved in going to see a production of which they had not heard. The survey showed that the specially produced *How Much?* print had been effective in encouraging young people to attend, however focus groups revealed that with more information and clearer messages its effectiveness could be further increased.

It is vital that the learning outcomes of the *How Much?* project are built upon in the future to ensure that the new audiences gained are retained.

1.9   Recommendations

▶ increase the minimum price of less well-known productions to £5.00 for young people aged 16-24 years. This reflects a fairly high willingness to pay more among the survey respondents. For better-known productions, there is little need for a drastic price discount because the popularity of the performance will ensure that young people will pay more.

▶ continue to provide a season brochure specific to young people, designed in consultation with young people.

▶ ensure that promotional materials for less well-known productions contain as much information as possible regarding the performance.

▶ target marketing towards those market segments that have been shown by this research to have low attendance rates at the theatre, such as: 22 to 24-year-olds, unemployed people, college students and males.

▶ target incentives to attend the theatre - particularly those with the label 'young person' - primarily at 16 to 18 year olds.

RESULTS AND ANALYSIS OF *HOW MUCH?* NON-ATTENDERS SURVEY

2.1   Introduction

The non-attender survey was conducted with students in three weeks of term time in March 1999, by a team of leisure management postgraduate students from The University of Sheffield. The sample of survey respondents was selected randomly, completing self-administered questionnaires at communal facilities on campuses of The University of Sheffield and Sheffield College (a further education college). Those who had attended Sheffield Theatres previously were filtered out with a preliminary question. A total of 554 non-attender students were surveyed, 318 from The University of Sheffield and 236 from Sheffield College.

2.2   Non-attender survey respondents' characteristics

The sample was taken from the student community, the one that dominates the user survey sample and that at the outset was felt most likely to respond to the project. The low proportion of 22 to 24-year-olds in the user survey is explained by the low proportion of students in this category, as shown in Table 2.1.

Age	%
16 - 18 years	38
19 -21 years	38
22 - 24 years	17
>24 years	7
Gender	**%**
Female	54
Male	46
Education	**%**
FE College	43
University	57

▲ | *Table 2.1 - non-attender survey characteristics*

2.3 Programming and place

2.3.1 Perceptions of theatres

The young non-attenders surveyed gave a mix of perceptions about theatres generally as a product, in response to an open question. These perceptions are summarised in Table 2.2. They show a broad balance of positive, neutral and negative attitudes.

▼ Table 2.2 - non-attenders'
perceptions of theatres

Type of comment	No.	Examples of responses to 'Theatres are...?'
General		**(number of responses)**
positive	43	'interesting' (5), 'great' (5), 'entertaining' (6) 'a nice change from the American rubbish at the cinema'
neutral	23	'OK, if you're in the mood' (2) 'requiring a certain degree of concentration and interest'
negative	36	'boring' (15), 'not very interesting' (6) 'a place to go for a good sleep'
Performance		
positive	7	'a whole variety of entertainment' (4) 'useful ... to feel as though you are participating in the plot'
neutral	23	'good if there's something on that appeals to me' (17) 'good, but it is hard to find out which plays are good and which aren't'
negative	10	'there is usually nothing on that I am interested in' (4) 'not very entertaining - prefer the blood and violence of the big screen'
Price		
neutral	17	'good but often expensive' (9) 'in need of price subsidies to encourage the younger generation of TV addicts'
negative	24	'expensive' (20) 'out of my price range'
Educational		
positive	21	'an educational and cultural night out' (7) 'places where people can be moved and perhaps learn to understand experiences and emotions alien to their own lives'
neutral	4	'where we used to go on school trips' (2)
Social		
positive	19	'a good night out' (9) 'a different night out (7)
neutral	18	'good night out but not something I would normally do' (7) 'places to go with your mum and dad'
negative	13	'for older people' (8) 'places other people go'
Class		
negative	17	'visited by mainly upper class people' (7) 'stuffy and generally attended by art based people'
Experience		
neutral	8	'don't know, I haven't been there' (5)
negative	2	'not really for me and I don't know what's on'

2.3.2 Programme

Non-attenders identified a wide range of types of production that they would be interested in attending, from a list of prompted responses provided in the question, as shown in Table 2.3. This suggests that it was not programming which was the major constraint preventing their attendance.

Generally the significantly larger potential markets were females and university students. Different age segments have different preferences, with pantomimes appealing particularly to 16 to 18 - year-olds, West End* shows to 19 to 21-year-olds, and plays to 22 to 24-year-olds.

2.4 Promotion

2.4.1 Awareness of How Much?

Only 13% of the non-attenders surveyed had heard of the How Much? project. 87% had not. The lack of awareness was even higher for 16-21-year-olds (91%) and FE college non-attenders (92%). Of the minority who had heard of the How Much? project, 38% found out from posters and 24% from the How Much? leaflet. Surprisingly few (10%) had found out by word of mouth.

2.4.2 Promotion media used

Table 2.4 opposite summarises the promotion means used by non-attenders to find information about leisure activities. It demonstrates the importance of word of mouth, which echoes findings from the user survey.

▼| Table 2.3 - productions identified as either 'very attractive' or 'attractive' to non-attenders

Production	All	Female	Male	FE coll.	Univ.	16-18	19-20	22-24
	% of respondents citing "very attractive" or "attractive"							
Play	47	57	37	32	59	35	55	59
West End show*	42	50	34	34	48	41	48	35
Play studied at school	37	43	30	28	43	34	39	43
Musical	33	43	22	25	39	27	38	37
Pantomime	28	31	25	38	21	38	24	16
Ballet	17	27	5	7	24	8	20	27
Contemporary dance	16	22	11	15	17	16	15	16
Opera	13	18	8	9	17	7	18	15

*The meaning of the term 'West End Show' was left to the respondent to interpret, but was intended to mean a play or musical known for its previous success in London's West End.

Promotion means	All	FE coll.	Univ.	16-18	19-20	22-24
% of respondents citing 'very useful' or 'useful'						
Personal recommendation	68	49	81	59	74	72
Posters	50	45	54	46	52	60
Leaflets	39	30	45	32	47	46
Newspapers	37	39	35	32	38	46
Radio	33	48	22	50	24	18

◀ Table 2.4 - promotion means identified as 'very useful' or 'useful' by non-attenders

There are significant differences in the popularity of different promotion means, by age and by the type of student. Personal recommendation was much more important to university students. Posters and leaflets increased in importance with age of young person, and are more important to university students. Radio was clearly more important to the youngest segment and FE college students - possibly because they are more likely to have been brought up locally and they listen more to local radio.

2.4.3 Incentives

When asked about the extent to which different types of incentive would attract them to attend the theatre, the product (in the shape of the types of production and well-known actors) emerges as the most important type of incentive.

There were some significant differences in the importance of different incentives, by gender, age and type of education, although for all market segments the product-related incentives of 'plays interested in' and 'well-known actors' were attractive to the highest proportion of non-attenders.

Incentives	All	Female	Male	FE coll.	Univ.	16-18	19-20	22-24
% of respondents citing 'very attractive' or 'attractive'								
Play interested in	76	77	75	62	86	66	81	86
Well known actors	64	67	61	63	65	63	66	68
Low price	60	66	54	54	64	60	59	65
Ticket deals	51	59	43	42	59	46	59	49
Free drink, programmes, etc.	49	51	47	51	48	54	48	49
Pre & post show entertainment	40	40	41	43	39	43	39	44

▲ Table 2.5 - incentives identified as either 'very attractive' or 'attractive' to non-attenders

2.5 Price

2.5.1 Perceptions of cost

Non-attenders were asked, 'Do you think theatres are expensive?' 78% said 'yes', (this is considerably higher than the equivalent finding for users) 22% said 'no'. Female non-attenders (83%) and FE college students (81%) were more likely to view theatres as expensive.

2.5.2 Price as a constraint

When asked, 'Why haven't you visited Sheffield Theatres?', respondents rated the importance of a number of constraints, [see Table 2.6]. The most widespread was the perception that Sheffield Theatres are 'too expensive' - this is consistent with the importance of price/money constraints for users. The relative importance of the time constraint for non-attenders was similar to users.

Constraints	All	Female	Male	FE coll.	Univ.	16-18	19-20	22-24
	% of respondents citing 'very important' or 'important'							
Too expensive	48	56	39	52	46	50	52	46
Not sure what's on	43	42	45	32	51	42	42	50
High work load	42	47	35	37	45	42	43	40
Not enough time	40	48	31	36	43	40	39	43
Not interested	37	29	46	49	28	49	32	23
No one to go with	23	26	20	23	23	26	22	20
Lack of transport	15	16	13	16	14	20	12	9

▲ Table 2.6 - how non attenders rated constraints

Once again, there were some significant differences in the importance of different constraints for non-attenders of different ages, gender and education type. Expense was particularly relevant to females, FE college students and to younger market segments. Lack of awareness was the most extensive constraint for university students. Lack of interest was the top constraint for males and the second highest constraint for FE college students and 16-18-year-olds.

2.5.3   Willingness to pay

66% of non-attenders surveyed said they would be willing to pay between £3 and £9.99, with 23% willing to pay less than £3 and 11% willing to pay £10 or more. This result is broadly in line with the audience survey findings. FE college students and 16 to 18-year-olds were least willing to pay more - 34% and 29% respectively were not willing to pay more than £3. It should be noted that individuals' answers to such a question could be cautious, leading to an overall underestimate of willingness to pay.

2.5.4   Leisure expenditure

Average weekly spending on leisure by non-attenders was similar to that found in the attenders' survey, with 54% spending £45 or more per week. Nonetheless, there was a substantial minority, 28%, spending less than £20 a week on leisure, as with the attenders. This low spending minority was bigger in FE colleges (36%), and in the 16-18-year-old segment (36%). Despite the large minority with low spending, the results confirm the impression from the attender survey - that money was not an absolute constraint for many young people. Instead, relative to other leisure activities, the theatre was more susceptible to financial considerations by young people in making the attendance choice, possibly because of uncertainties about the benefits that they will get from the production.

2.6   Conclusions and recommendations

It is clear that what attracts young non-attenders to try the theatre is the combination of price, product and promotion.

▶ the most common view was that going to the theatre is expensive. This perception was the most important constraint for young people. The normal *How Much?* price of £3.50 was seen by many as rather low, with £5 being acceptable to the majority.

▶ it was the plays and shows themselves that were the most likely to attract non-attenders to the theatre. These non-attenders were interested in a wide range of productions.

▶ approximately seven out of eight non-attenders had not heard of the *How Much?* project by March 1999, six months after the *pilot phase* had started.

These results endorse the original marketing plan of the *How Much?* project, which incorporated price, product and promotion changes. Any continuing initiative at Sheffield Theatres directed at young people needs to ensure an appropriate marketing mix.

The survey of young non-attenders has revealed a lot of market segmentation information. There are significant differences in perceptions, constraints and potential responses to incentives to attend by different types of young people. Any continuing initiative directed at young people in Sheffield Theatres should use this information to target more accurately both 'softer' targets with high market potential (e.g. females, university students) and more difficult targets such as young males and FE college students.

INVESTIGATION INTO 'GATEKEEPERS' VIEWS ON YOUNG PEOPLE'S ATTENDANCE AT THE THEATRE.

3.1   Introduction

The aim of this investigation was to find out more about why and how teachers, youth leaders and lecturers encourage individuals or groups of young people to attend Sheffield Theatres. Short questionnaires were sent by Elizabeth Owen of Sheffield Hallam University to heads of English and Drama in schools, and also to city-wide services and area youth leaders in Sheffield. The research objective was to investigate the role of professionals working with groups of young people in supporting young people's attendance at Sheffield Theatres.

Personal and telephone interviews were undertaken with selected respondents to the questionnaires, and lecturers at Sheffield Colleges. This is a summary of the findings to date with information on:

▶ the form their encouragement takes
▶ why they do it
▶ their responses to recent visits to Sheffield Theatres
▶ ways in which Sheffield Theatres could support their encouragement of young people's attendance at the theatres

In all, 15 'gatekeepers' have contributed to this investigation. All had arranged a visit by a group of young people to the theatre within the past two years.

3.2 People

The professionals who were interviewed are in a position to act as personal intermediaries or, as one respondent suggested,

"ticket agents - leaders into the arts garden".

Thus the term 'gatekeeper' was used to identify this group of people. Gatekeepers, within teaching, youth work and lecturing are not a homogeneous group, nor are the young people with whom they work. Teachers' motivation was the curriculum. Practice in schools varied. There was awareness that pupils not studying set texts for examinations should not be denied the experience of going to the theatre and appropriate performances were selected. Youth leaders were motivated to take groups to shows which offered 'a good night out' or were relevant to young people and could be used in support of issue-based youth work, or to explore a particular group's concerns. For example, one leader said,

"the main issue is one of relevance, particularly where Asian young people are concerned".

Youth workers also revealed two other influences on their support of young people's attendance: their own enjoyment of theatre and the creation of an appropriate opportunity to enable young people to do something they may not have previously experienced. The lecturers' motivation was seeking opportunities for young people to experience professional practice of subjects being studied, be it dance, drama or venue management.

3.3 Place

Teachers, lecturers and youth leaders identified their role in introducing young people to the new experience of attending a performance at the theatre. All mentioned the support they offered to young people about: what to expect, appropriate behaviour so as not to disrupt other members of the audience, and audience conventions, such as not talking to each other, not using mobile phones and not walking in and out of the auditorium during a performance. Teachers included the study of texts in this preparation. Youth leaders noted the importance of the process of negotiation with young people in the selection of a performance, suggesting issues for discussion, deciding to attend and, finally, participating. Lecturers linked the visit with the area of study. All recognised that they could not expect a visit to the theatre to be part of participants' previous experience. All sought to ensure that the experience was positive. The suggestion was made that, while in no way wishing to isolate the age group, a 'young people's night' might enable young people to have a less inhibited response to the performance. In their work all dealt with the evaluation of participants' responses to the experience. One respondent felt that the theatres did not have 'enough appreciation of what it means to stimulate arts interests in [disadvantaged] children'. The availability of transport for groups of young people to the theatre varied. Youth leaders' access to minibuses varied. Teachers noted that matinee performances took away the difficulty of transporting young people late at night.

3.4 Programming

Teachers, lecturers and youth leaders identified their role as selectors of appropriate product for young people. Selection of product was influenced by the curriculum, issues relevant to young people, and area of study. Attendance at performance-related talks, discussions, workshops offered by the theatres was influenced by the relevance to these three areas. Youth groups commented that while they had not always understood the content of some shows because of difficulties with the plot or strangeness of live performance, members had enjoyed visits because of the experience of a special night out and the theatrical spectacle.

3.5 Promotion

Not everyone received publicity material about the theatres. Those who did displayed it so young people and other colleagues could have access to it. Unspecific criticism of the inflexibility of the theatre's group booking system was made. In one case, lack of advance detailed information about the content of a particular production had led to distress amongst a youth group with special needs. This led to the suggestion that the timely production of more detailed information for people working with young people could support gatekeepers in their promotion of visits to the theatre. Advance publicity was not always available when curriculum and activity planning were taking place. Teachers said that the information given in publicity was adequate, but youth leaders felt that further detail about performances might help them. The respondents all felt that the work undertaken by gatekeepers organising visits to the theatres should not be underestimated.

3.6 Price

The total cost of a visit to the theatre was thought by all to be expensive. To arrange visits to the theatre, teachers, youth leaders and in some cases lecturers would have to raise funds from other sources to pay for or subsidise the cost to participants. Other sources of funds were not readily available. Advance knowledge was needed to plan and apply for funds. It was acknowledged that group discounts, concessionary prices and special offers available through the theatres helped put ticket prices within reach, the respondents suggested a price range of £2-£5. The cost of transport, programmes and refreshments had to be considered, as did the cost for the legally required number of accompanying adults. The gatekeepers' practice of dealing with the additional costs differed. As the experience of attending the theatre was frequently unknown to potential participants, gatekeepers found there was often a reluctance to make a small financial contribution. The work of gatekeepers in fund-raising and collecting contributions was also noted.

3.7 Conclusion

In conclusion Sheffield Theatres were asked to consider:

▶ the timing, content and distribution of special promotional material to gatekeepers
▶ the group booking system
▶ the time of performances
▶ special performances for young people
▶ opportunities for gatekeepers themselves to experience and enjoy attendance at the theatres to improve their understanding of performances

FURTHER RESEARCH NEEDS ARISING FROM THE MONITORING OF THE *HOW MUCH?* PROJECT.

Although the monitoring of the *How Much?* project has been extensive, it is still possible to identify further research which would be useful in informing further policies of this type.

4.1

Longitudinal qualitative and quantitative research exploring:

▶ for how long the diminution in the perception that 'theatres are expensive' lasts as a result of *How Much?* prices, and how quickly the perception is affected by changes in prices

▶ for how long the high percentage of visits which are first visits can be sustained, and the relationship between this percentage and pricing changes

▶ the extent to which repeat visits take place by those young people who first visited Sheffield Theatres as part of the *How Much?* project, and how pricing changes affect repeat visiting.

All of this information would directly inform pricing policy in relation to young people.

4.2

Qualitative research to explore in more depth why many young people spend a considerable amount of money on leisure, yet claim 'not enough money' and 'ticket prices too high' are important constraints to visiting the theatre. This would hopefully resolve the apparent inconsistency in the evidence from the current research and thus help Sheffield Theatres to increase the effectiveness with which it attracts and retains young people.

4.3

Survey research to investigate audiences at Sheffield Theatres other than young people and particularly their reaction to the *How Much?* project. Are there, for instance, any conflicts of interest between young people and other market segments and can these be accommodated in pricing, promotion or programming policy? This question derives from a few anecdotal incidents of complaint, by people not of the age group covered by the *How Much?* price concessions; they felt they were, in effect, being discriminated against.

4.4

Survey research of young people at non-*How Much?* performances to identify the extent and type of young people attending at normal prices; and their awareness of and attitude to special initiatives such as the *How Much?* project. This would help Sheffield Theatres to reflect on whether a 'blanket' policy for the 16-24 year market segment is appropriate, or whether further market segmentation within this age group might be worthwhile.

4.5

Qualitative research exploring in more depth the effects of the *How Much?* project on, and attitudes to the theatre by, more 'difficult' young target groups, both attenders and non-attenders, such as males, less educated, unemployed, those 'at risk' of offending, etc. These groups are not well represented in the current research. To complement this, qualitative research with appropriate gatekeepers is needed.

4.6

Quantitative research to identify more formally the price elasticity of demand by young people in relation to Sheffield Theatres; and the consequent effects of price discount initiatives on the theatres' revenue. This would embrace a comparison of special initiatives such as *How Much?* with other initiatives such as the young persons' membership, and the use of standby tickets. Combined with the research into how long the beneficial effects of the *How Much?* project last [See 4.1], this research would provide evidence of the sustainability of initiatives such as *How Much?* i.e. the extent to which they can be maintained through time. The research could also extend to the effects of price discounts on other non-attending target groups, such as those on low incomes.

Section 5

Artistic development

D2K and 23:59

Huw Chadbourn and Lysette Anthony in **23:59** *written by Nicola Baldwin*

Introduction

The *How Much?* project had a multi-pronged approach to developing new audiences. Part of it consisted of the programming, marketing and research described in sections 3 and 4 of this report. Part of it was also the D2K **group and the commissioning of a new play,** 23:59**. Together, these ventures and some work by the Sheffield Theatres marketing and education departments with schools and colleges comprised an artistic development scheme.**

The aims of the artistic development scheme were:

▶ to commission and stage a play aimed at young people and specific to Sheffield and to the interests of the 16 to 24-years-age group - the play and the writer

▶ to bring together a group of around 12-16 young people, and involve them over a period of months as makers of work, shapers of publicity for the target audience and networkers to help create new younger audiences - the key group

▶ to support young artists by offering six-month attachments for two young artists to make their own work, and to work with the key group, sharing their creativity and acting as role models - the artists in residence

▶ to make the introduction of the key group's presence in Sheffield Theatres a catalyst to opening up communications within the theatre and to fostering an accessible atmosphere for young people in Sheffield to attend the theatre and feel involved with its work

▶ to create a post of dramaturg/project coordinator to commission and work with the writer, to initiate and manage the artistic programme and to oversee the work of the key group and the artists in residence - the dramaturg

The artistic development scheme outlined above was initially called Disco 2000, after the song by Pulp, and became shortened to D2K

The dramaturg

In December 1998, Louise Mulvey was appointed to the post of dramaturg/project coordinator. It was stressed that for the project to work the holder of this post would have to liaise with the education and the marketing departments of the theatres and ensure that staff throughout Sheffield Theatres were aware of and connected with the processes of the play and of the key group. Sheffield Theatres had never had a dramaturg (literary manager) or a producer/project manager before.

Louise Mulvey had previously been working as director of North West Playwrights, lobbying for and developing award-winning writers in the region, and had a background in dramaturgy and also in script-reading for, among others, the Royal National Theatre, the Arts Council and the BBC World Service.

Mulvey began work in February 1999 and recalls: 'the ideas behind D2K represented everything I believe about contemporary theatre. That theatre must be relevant and exciting to an audience, and that if a theatre company is to fulfill a function as the voice of a community, a writer must be present to hear and retell the stories of that community.' Mulvey's first step was to pin a definition of a dramaturg to her office door.

Selecting the writer, the key group and the artists in residence

Three writers came forward for consideration; two pulled out - the project was seen as high risk, especially given a relatively large venue for a new work and less than glamorous remuneration. Nicola Baldwin began work in March 1999. She is an experienced playwright whose first taste of theatre as a child was at The Crucible. She has worked for television as well as for theatres such as Royal National Theatre, London, Royal Exchange, Manchester and at the Edinburgh Fringe. She is also writing tutor at the Royal Court Theatre's young writers' programme.

In approaching colleges, training organisations and youth agencies in search of members of the key group, the education department and the dramaturg looked out for 'self-starters', who could be articulate, inventive and able to work cooperatively.

It took longer than expected to assemble the group and was hard to find enough males. Workshop sessions were run by the education department, not only to help select, but also to give applicants a taste of what might be to come. In the 12 people selected, there were four young men and eight young women, mostly aged 19-21. Some were still at college, some already graduates. Some were involved in existing arts organisation training, such as community arts projects or music studios.

From among ten possibles, performance artist Rachael Walton and graphic designer Jimmy Turrell were selected as artists in residence. They were judged to be people who would be comfortable with having others watch them work, would not mind making mistakes in front of others and would like people, not only art. Mulvey tried to keep staff at the theatres updated with the progress of the project and to engender in them a stake in the success. She recalled:

"I had a sense of creating a new language - of inventing concepts and vocabulary in order to teach them to others.

"We held a big staff meeting in April to introduce the artists and Nicola and also to represent the project to the rest of the staff, I created a champagne pyramid with tap water and a box of glasses I begged from the bemused bar staff. The water represents Art and the tiers of glasses, the people involved in the project, from the artists and writer at the top to the D2K group to the staff, audience and wider community.

"I introduced the experiment to a wary, slightly cynical meeting, craved their indulgence and started pouring. Do people think I'm mad? Are they ready to engage? Will they remember this comment on the dissemination of creativity in Sheffield Theatres? Time will tell".

The key group: progress and evaluation

The key group began work, meeting about once a week, with the alternating presence of the two artists. They had a contract and a set of aims and objectives, but putting these into practice proved very challenging, when no-one knew what the outcomes would be and it all felt very risky. Sometimes Mulvey arranged for them to go and see shows.

They created two websites, on D2K itself and on 23:59, the play that was being written. A fanzine was also produced and distributed.

A theatre piece - Trashed - was written, with Rachael's help, and produced in the Studio in August. Rachael explained,

"The idea was for the group to work together to create something to encourage other young people into the Crucible and show how the building can be accessible. I thought it would be interesting to create an atmosphere that would transfer the place into something more like a club than a theatre."

Trashed followed a group of young people on a night out where language, dress codes, drinking and drugs dictate social conventions and expected modes of behaviour. The production incorporated video, slide projection, a live DJ and voice-over. It was very popular.

D2K was not without its problems. Tensions focused around a number of issues, such as editorial content of the work and relationships with other people and departments in the theatres. The 'link scheme' envisaged as a way of building bridges between individuals in the key group and individuals in various departments of the theatres, through a 'buddy' system, was more or less a non-starter. Staff are comfortable and experienced with young people on work placements or shadowing schemes. But the link scheme lacked focus - the **D2K** members did not always keep appointments or realise that staff had other commitments. Perhaps the staff should have been more flexible, perhaps the key group members could have been be more structured, in their approach to time-keeping.

The artists in residence:
progress and evaluation
Jimmy Turrell, a graphic artist, was not long out of college, had little experience of the culture of organisations, professional life and the theatre. But he adapted quickly and moved his workplace into the theatre, where he met increasing demands for his contribution. He created posters and leaflets for 23:59 and other publicity as well as cooperating in other ways with the education department and with the marketing team. Rachael Walton, performance artist, lives in Sheffield and this proved a great asset in many ways. She was however, involved with other projects as well as D2K and was very busy.

The writer:
progress and evaluation
The diversity of aims attributed to D2K did not perhaps impinge on the writer, Nicola Baldwin, as much as on the others. [See pages 63-65]

The dramaturg/project coordinator:
progress and evaluation
The creation of the post of dramaturg/project coordinator was intended to drive forward the different elements of the artistic development package. Louise Mulvey's job description contained not only a dramaturg's focus on developing a script, honing ideas with the writer and bringing the finished article to the stage, but also a project coordinator's responsibility for shepherding the D2K young artists, enabling them to produce work and facilitating their communication with staff.

Sheffield Theatres had not had the services of a dramaturg before. Nor had the theatre staff worked with young artists in quite the way proposed by D2K. Unsurprisingly, the diversity of the project's aims and the different expectations of those involved created some tensions. In many respects, the process was one of continual negotiation of roles and relationships from February to December 1999. By the latter stages of the project, this process had borne fruit in that there was a greater understanding of the dramaturg's role, the role of the key group and the purpose of 23:59.

The project took some positive steps to address the fear of the new. For example, the theatres' education department and the dramaturg devised 'awareness sessions' for the permanent staff on the experience of young people in Sheffield Theatres, both as new attendees and as young artists. Three sessions involved a mix of staff from different departments - catering, box office, front of house, production, marketing and senior management. The groups were given the opportunity to regress to their teenage years, with discussion on:

▶ the first record/CD I bought
▶ my favourite item of clothing when I was a teenager
▶ something about me that might surprise you

Having broken the ice, groups were then put in unfamiliar surroundings, such as a greyhound track for those who'd never been, and asked to list what they would need to know and how they would like to be treated to feel more comfortable in a strange environment. The groups were asked to carry out these exercises first as customers, and then as staff. The sessions were well-attended and positively received by staff, who described them as 'thought-provoking' and 'useful'.

The impact of D2K on the theatres as an organisation
One of the aims of the D2K project was to address the role of artists in the building and to encourage staff members to appreciate the creative process that their work supports. It was also hoped that having the key group as a regular presence in the building would have a positive effect on the attitudes of theatre

staff towards young people, whether as young artists or young audience. As Mulvey reflected: 'there's no point spending all this time and money getting young people into the building if they are not made to feel welcome when they arrive'.

There was a sense that the project was being continually judged against financial criteria - 'was D2K value for money?' With a project designed to be experimental and creative this pressure was not helpful. As with other elements of the project, the demand to produce measurable results from the earliest stage could have been counter productive to a process which aimed for a longer-term developmental approach.

This account of D2K, which draws almost entirely upon a report drafted by the dramaturg, Louise Mulvey, may seem rather downbeat. Mulvey is, however, very positive about the benefits of D2K, both in the present and the future. Reflecting on how it felt in the midst of the project, with tight deadlines and a need to ask favours of many people, she observed: 'given the layers of the project, each involving different people and each piloting an idea, the extent to which things are clear and engaged is quite remarkable'. Many of the benefits are bound to be hard to quantify. Identifying these tensions is not intended as a criticism of Sheffield Theatres or of the individuals concerned. It is important to understand that any project concerned with development - be it audience or artistic development - is primarily concerned with change. And the process of change can be threatening.

Conclusion

It is clear that D2K presented a fantastic opportunity for young artists involved. They were encouraged to make art, try out ideas, taste the experience of working in a professional atmosphere and attend an extraordinarily rich mixture of plays and performance. One of the meanings of the word crucible is 'severe test or trial' and in that sense, D2K offered almost everyone concerned, not only a challenge, and a testing but also, if that was appropriate, a wake-up.

A play for *How Much?* - 23:59

An important part of *How Much?* was the commissioning and staging of a play that would be relevant and exciting for audiences aged 16-24. This element of the project ran alongside all the other strands of work - the research, the targeting, the outreach and publicity and the D2K group. It was intended that the play would be a catalyst for developing a sustained growth of interest in theatre among young people in and around Sheffield.

The process.

Playwright Nicola Baldwin was commissioned by Sheffield Theatres in February 1999 and began work soon after. Nicola's task was not only to write a play to a brief provided by Sheffield Theatres, but also to write it in time for it to be staged in the Crucible in the autumn. What's more, she was asked to work alongside dramaturg Louise Mulvey, and to welcome the involvement of D2K's group of 12 young people.

If this were not daunting enough, there was the prospect of filling the 980-seat Crucible with an audience for a new play: this is an incredible challenge when, for the most part, new writing in Britain is staged in studio venues of 100-200 seats.

The concept of the play, summarised in a document produced by Deborah Paige (Sheffield Theatres artistic director) at the outset of the venture, was to:

▶ ask difficult questions about the post-industrial period in Sheffield

▶ focus on the last 25 years of the music scene, particularly on the female experience

▶ tell a story in which the main protagonists are young women.

With an audience much more used to the narrative of film than theatre, the brief was to draw on the possibilities of music and spectacle, and not to be afraid of emotional content.

By June, Nicola Baldwin had produced a first draft, which she presented to the D2K young artists for their comments and ideas. The deadlines for all aspects of the production were fairly hair-raising. Sheffield Theatres was in the position of commissioning a play with a firm commitment to staging it in the autumn season - an exceptional situation compared to the usual process of commissioning. The writer and the dramaturg began to work in earnest - a matter of chemistry as well as commitment and skills. At the same time, publicity materials such as leaflets and posters were in preparation.

Billed as 'a story of ambition, and revenge in the music industry, set at the biggest party Sheffield's ever had' (millennium eve), 23:59 opened on 5 November and ran for 18 performances. As dramaturg, Louise Mulvey reflected, 'the young people who came enjoyed the play and appreciated the effort that had gone into creating work for them.'

The critics

The hostility of the critics was a surprise and a disappointment. The *Daily Telegraph* headline, 'The cutting edge is blunt in Sheffield', was followed by the opinion that the play offered a 'dire and patronising evening'. Little allowance was made for the risk-taking involved or the commitment and faith being shown by Sheffield Theatres in staging the play for three weeks in its main auditorium

Fortunately, some critics were able to see 23:59 as part of the bigger picture - the need to develop new young audiences for British theatre. Lynda Murdin, theatre critic of the *Yorkshire Post*, had been following the *How Much?* project since its inception. Although her review of 23:59 was not glowing, she managed some praise for the 'interesting characters [and] occasionally well-honed scenes.'

In an interview with Angela Galvin as part of the *How Much?* evaluation exercise, Murdin outlined her view that the perceived elitism of theatre has diminished over the past five years, possibly creating an environment where projects like *How Much?* and productions like **23:59** have more chance of success. She also expressed a concern that gaining young audiences might be at the expense of older ones: 'The audience for some of your productions has been teeming with young people. It has to be a good thing, to encourage them away from solitary activity, like computer games, and into the communal experience of live art. But', she asks, 'is that off-putting to your older audience? And is it certain that young people want theatres to segregate them?'

Murdin praised Sheffield Theatres' earlier production of Mojo, and 23:59 as avoiding the pitfalls of 'attracting young people by appealing to the lowest common denominators of sex and violence.' She praised the way that both Mojo and 23:59 featured elements of sex and violence, 'but left it to our imaginations.' Murdin concluded by stating that, even though she hadn't wholeheartedly enjoyed 23:59, if viewed as a 'work in progress' it was a valuable contribution,

"a good idea...something different."

Conclusion

'Given the experimental nature of the project and the fact that it was designed to create a new audience, the fact that anyone came is impressive,' said Mulvey. 'Audiences averaging 92 per performance may feel small in such a large theatre, but in most venues where new work is produced they would have felt comfortable and even sold out.'

Commissioning and staging 23:59 was an important element of the *How Much?* project, bearing witness to Sheffield Theatres' willingness to try out new things and take risks in the quest to find out what young audiences want and appeal to them in new ways.

23:59 has recently been nominated for the prestigious Susan Smith Blackburn Award, 2000.

Section 6

Conclusion and recommendations

Una Stubbs in **Twelfth Night** *written by William Shakespeare*

The *How Much?* project was a response to the government's pledge to support wider access to the arts. The project's primary focus was on how the mix of programming, price and promotion affects young people's attendance of theatre.

A survey sample of more than 1,500 young people, together with the box office records of over 32,000 ticket sales provided some answers. Other questions were raised during the project - questions about why theatre needs new audiences and what theatre can offer new audiences in return. The project's efforts to answer these questions have recognised not only the commercial impact of growing an audience, but also the emotional and social impact on both artists and audiences. The *How Much?* project, its conclusions and recommendations have been generated by our genuine belief in the value of live theatre as a basis for interpreting and enriching our lives. Sheffield Theatres and our partners in the *How Much?* project see access to artistic life as a mainstay of the longer-term agenda of social inclusion for all young people.

Having a good time is important to young people, but the notion that attracting young people requires a 'dumbing down' of the artistic programme is challenged by some of the *How Much?* findings. Drama is a consistently popular form - particularly if the subject matter is relevant, or if it presents an insight to issues outside the audience's own experience. Spectacle and a sense of occasion can also counteract risk and challenge - more than 70% of the young audience would have paid more to see both the Maly Theatre's production of The Winter's Tale (in Russian) and Sheffield Theatres' production of Angels in America [See Recommendation 1].

In targeting young people on low incomes, Sheffield Theatres' was acknowledging that this significant segment of the city's population was under-represented in its audiences. From the earliest stages, our ability to greatly reduce the cost of theatre-going - when combined with targeted programming - had an immediate impact. We gained an audience of 12,000 young people in the *pilot phase* alone. 93% of the first-time attenders felt 'encouraged to return' to the theatre. Our challenge now is to develop a sustainable pricing policy, addressing the research finding that theatre is subject to more financial scrutiny than any other leisure expenditure. [See Recommendations 2 and 3].

Young people are not a homogeneous group. The preferences expressed within the *How Much?* sample by age, by occupation and by gender suggest that different approaches are necessary in order to attract different segments of the young audience. Pricing and programming decisions to attract these segments need to be communicated effectively. The *How Much?* project gave some insights into the marketing activities that worked best across the segment. We now have not only the task of integrating these activities with the theatres' general marketing plans but also the challenge of attempting to influence the most significant marketing communication - word of mouth.
[See Recommendation 4].

The time limits of the project militated against developing qualitative relationships with some of the more difficult to reach segments of our target group. However, we were able to forge partnerships with organisations that will enable us to reach young people in these segments beyond the project's lifespan.
[See Recommendation 5].

Increasing the proportion of young people in our audience by 34% in a matter of months was rewarding. But there were suggestions that this increase was achieved at the expense of the quality of experience for some older audience members. Some of these issues are simply those of 'theatre etiquette', such as not using a mobile phone in the auditorium, and can easily be addressed. But young people, teachers, lecturers, youth leaders and the core audience have expressed contradictory views about the links between some of the 'etiquette' issues and young people's need to establish identity and a sense of belonging in unfamiliar surroundings. We remain uncertain about the relative benefits of segregating young audiences or integrating them.
[See Recommendations 6 and 7].

Sheffield Theatres took risks in programming (e.g. Angels in America, 23:59), in pricing (e.g. supporting a 'loss' in box office income of up to £11 per ticket) and in promotion (e.g. investment in a website, testing focus group feedback by producing varied marketing communications). These risks were effectively underwritten by the New Audiences scheme. Without the scheme, little of the activity outlined in this report could have taken place. [See Recommendation 8].

Some of the *How Much?* project's findings are generalisable to the work of other arts organisations. Some may be specific to Sheffield and its theatres. Others require further testing before they are applied to practice or included in policy. Clearly, a time-limited project - even one that generates 32,000+ ticket sales, 29% of which were to first-time attenders - cannot answer all the questions raised by the issue of growing young people's theatre attendance. Nonetheless, we do feel that the project has made a significant contribution to the debate. Sheffield Theatres' claim to be in a unique position to carry out audience development work targeted at young people has been strengthened by the achievements of *How Much?*

Recommendation 1

Sheffield Theatres should use the research findings on 'attractive' productions as headlines for developing a strand of artistic programming that has a clear, accessible and honest vision for young audiences.

Recommendation 2

Sheffield Theatres should continue its partnership with The University of Sheffield and Sheffield Hallam University to conduct further research, over a longer period, to test the sustainability of price-led initiatives in attracting young audiences in general, and first-time attenders in particular.

Recommendation 3

Sheffield Theatres should implement a pilot pricing policy, targeting discounted tickets at those groups (e.g. 16 to 18-year-olds and young women) for whom price was shown to be a particular constraint.

Recommendation 4

Sheffield Theatres should attempt to influence word of mouth recommendations through a project to create young gatekeepers or ambassadors.

Recommendation 5

Sheffield Theatres should continue to develop partnerships with artists, statutory agencies and voluntary organisations to assert the centrality of theatre in initiatives to promote community development and social inclusion.

Recommendation 6

Sheffield Theatres should work with The University of Sheffield and Sheffield Hallam University to investigate the response of the core audience to pricing, promotion and programming policies that appear to favour young people.

Recommendation 7

Sheffield Theatres should pilot a 'young people only' night on one of its own productions in order to test the impact of a segregated performance on young people's attendance.

Recommendation 8

The Arts Council of England, and other bodies with an interest in including young people in this country's artistic life, should continue to support initiatives such as the *How Much?* project.

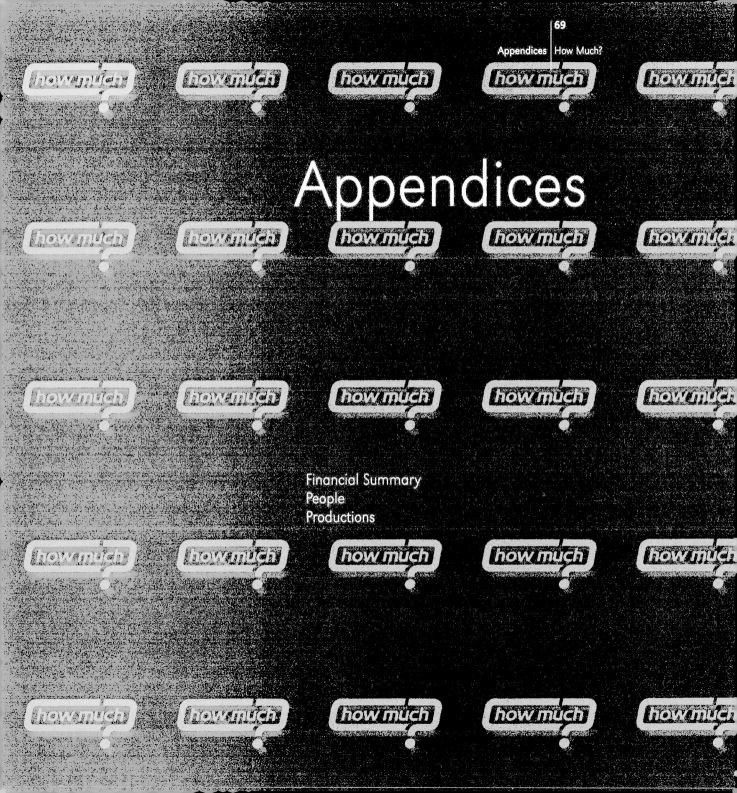

Appendices

Financial Summary
People
Productions

How Much? project expenditure

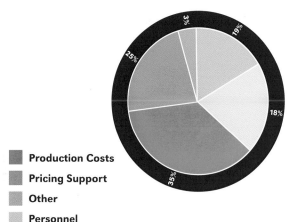

- Production Costs
- Pricing Support
- Other
- Personnel
- Marketing

How Much? project income

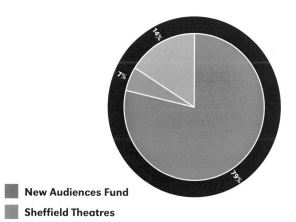

- New Audiences Fund
- Sheffield Theatres
- Partnership Support

Appendix 1
How Much? financial summary

Introduction

Sheffield Theatres' *How Much?* project had its own discrete budget and reporting regime. Project expenditure was spread across two financial years and was substantially underwritten by the New Audiences grant of £300,000, administered by the Arts Council of England. The remainder of the income, £77,525, was to be contributed by Sheffield Theatres Trust (STT) through its own fundraising efforts.

At the time the project was launched, detailed budgets were prepared for the *pilot phase* and *phase 1*. *Phases 2a* and *2b* remained less specific to allow for confirmation of programming, and adjustment for lessons learned in the earlier phases. The total cost was agreed from the start.

Budgets

Income budgets totalled £377,525.
Expenditure was split £183,800 in 1998/9 and £193,725 in 1999/2000.
Costs were grouped under: personnel [see Appendix 2] £60,825; marketing, £90,500; programme/production costs, £114,000; pricing support costs, £104,200; and other, £8,000.

▶ programme/production costs are contributions to the cost of producing a piece of work. For a Sheffield Theatres production (such as Mojo, Angels in America and 23:59) this amounts to a supplement enabling us to mount a production that might otherwise not be justifiable on cost grounds.

▶ pricing support costs represent the income to STT calculated by assuming all *How Much?* tickets were sold at the normal price*. For a visiting production this cost relates to the increase in the payment to the production company necessary to compensate for the low ticket prices. In practice this generally requires an additional payment to the producer based on a calculation assuming all tickets were sold at the normal price.

*In both instances 'normal' means after whatever discount would otherwise be applicable (e.g. student discounts).

Results
Final project figures showed

▶ New Audiences funding enabled Sheffield Theatres Trust to pursue artistic and audience development through programming work which would not otherwise have been financially feasible

▶ fewer resources were expended on marketing and production costs than originally budgeted

▶ the costs of pricing support were remarkably close to target

▶ fundraising was below target as the project was perceived as a risk - some potential supporters waited to see measurable results before committing funds

▶ severe delays in the administration of payments by the Arts Council. The initial budget provided for each phase to be funded in advance. This was the case for the *pilot phase* but *phases 1, 2a* and *2b* have been retrospectively funded - the final receipt for *phase1* being six months beyond the end of the phase. This has caused extreme cashflow difficulties which have only been manageable on the back of a financially successful year in 1998/9. Had the *How Much?* project taken place a year earlier it would probably have been insupportable in its final phase.

Appendix 2
People
How Much? project
co-ordinator, Haidee Bell (October 1998 - October 1999)
assistant, Kate Longworth (October 1998 - 1999)
research assistant, Sheffield Hallam University, Sophie Withnall (November 1998 - December 1999)

23:59
writer, Nicola Baldwin
dramaturg, Louise Mulvey (February - December 1999)
director, Sarah Frankcom
cast: Lysette Anthony, Kellie Bright, Huw Chadbourn, Kathryn Drysdale, Ian McHale, Harry Peacock, Lexi Strauss, Michael Vaughan.

Artists in residence
Rachael Walton
Jimmy Turrell

D2K key group
Gillian Capewell, Amy Golding, Anne Grange, Emily Keene, Georgina Kersey, Cathy Moggridge, Karen Mulcahey, Shane O'Connor, Andrew Reed, Adele Sellars, Joe Steyne, Tom Whitehead.

Steering group members
Angela Galvin, marketing and development director, Sheffield Theatres
Grahame Morris, chief executive, Sheffield Theatres
Louise Mulvey, *How Much?* project dramaturg
[William Nye, Department of Culture, Media and Sport]
Elizabeth Owen, Sheffield Hallam University
Emma Pratt, manager, The Forum
Professor Peter Taylor, The University of Sheffield
Professor Dianne Willcocks, principal, College of Ripon and York St. John

Funding partners
Advanced Digital Telecom
Arts Council of England
The Forum
The Freshgate Trust Foundation
Meadowhall Centre
Norwich Union
RJB Mining
Sheffield Hallam University
Sheffield Newspapers
The University of Sheffield
South Yorkshire Police
Westfield Contributory Health Scheme

Acknowledgments:
Annabel Dunbar, Andrew Godfrey (twentyfiveten design), Richard Hadley, Gareth Johnstone, Lynda Murdin, Gerry Murray, Dr Dominic Shellard, Pure Design, Simon Warner, Tracey Waters, Sheffield Theatres staff, and the producers, creative teams and acting companies of the productions listed in Appendix 3.

Appendix 3
How Much? productions
in chronological order - October 1998 to November 1999

A Clockwork Orange
written by Anthony Burgess
directed by Alan Lydiard and Mark Murphy
a Northern Stage production

One of this century's most controversial books and films is brought to frightening reality. Northern Stage animate the story of Alex and his teenage gang 'the droogs', their life of rape, murder and 'ultraviolence' and the moral dilemma that arises when Alex is brainwashed into good citizenship. Condemned as a glorification of violence and acclaimed as an indictment of state oppression. Make up your own mind. Projected film, a pounding soundtrack and 14 performers create a production that is definitely not for the fainthearted.

Popcorn
written by Ben Elton
directed by Laurence Boswell
a Phil McIntyre production

A brilliant and biting comedy about movie violence and the potential real life repercussions. Ben Elton's **Popcorn** is both a best-selling novel and an outrageously funny, gripping and thought-provoking play...When real life killers Wayne and Scout meet their idol, the award winning Tarantinoesque film director, Bruce Delamitri, the results are nothing short of explosive.

Twelfth Night
written by William Shakespeare
directed by Michael Grandage
a Sheffield Theatres production

A young countess in love with grief is courted by a young Duke who is in love with love. Their lives are invaded by a young girl who is in love with life. By the end of Shakespeare's great comedy the self-deceivers have all grown up. Supported by the antics of Sir Toby Belch, Sir Andrew Aguecheek, Malvolio, Maria and Feste the clown - a supreme cast of characters who've lost the plot!

Rambert Dance Company

Rambert Dance Company returns to Sheffield with a thrilling programme of contrasting dance by three of the world's top choreographers.
Merce Cunningham's *August Pace* - a series of light and elegant virtuoso duets.
Swansong - acclaimed as a classic. Created by Rambert's Artistic Director, Christopher Bruce.
Siobhan Davies' *Embarque* - performed to Steve Reich's tremendous surging score played live by the London Musici Orchestra.

Mojo

written by Jez Butterworth
directed by Deborah Paige
a Sheffield Theatres production

Welcome to the world of the Krays and Reservoir Dogs. Mojo mixes sex and drugs and rock 'n' roll with gang warfare and quickfire patter. Summer 1958. Rock 'n' roll has hit town and the place to be is Ezra's Atlantic Club, where rising star Silver Johnny - Britain's answer to Elvis - performs nightly to a crowd of ecstatic teenagers. *Mojo* is a tale of murder and betrayal told with explosive energy, fuelled by a startling and original use of language and music.

Macbeth

written by William Shakespeare
directed by John Crowley
a Thelma Holt and Karl Sydow production

Regarded by many as Shakespeare's greatest tragedy, *Macbeth* is as spellbinding today as it was for Elizabethan audiences. The lust for power puts flesh on the bones of a story in which power corrupts and absolute power corrupts absolutely. Macbeth's ambitions propel him swiftly towards the death of his queen, the loss of his kingdom and his own ultimate destruction.

Goodness Gracious Me

performed by Meera Syal, Kulvinder Ghir, Nina Wadia and Sanjeev Bhaskar
directed by Anil Gupta
a Phil McIntyre production

Rude boys and rude girls live on stage, innit? Emmy award nominated comedy as heard on radio, as seen on TV and now treading the boards.

Astor-Tango

performed by Gidon Kremer and the Kremerata Quartet with Vadim Sakharov, piano
a Music in the Round presentation

Gidon Kremer, one of the world's greatest violinists, lets his hair down in a tribute to the late king of tango, Astor Piazzolla. First the sexy tango, then an orgy of violins. Violin, piano, double bass and bandoneon range from haunting to romantic, from rigorous to melancholy. The discovery of Piazzolla is like finding some dangerous and exotic drug, a drug that could bring with it the double-edged sword of ecstasy and the bitterest remorse.

Sulphur 16

performed by Random Dance
directed by Wayne McGregor
a Danceworks 99 presentation

Sulphur 16 takes a fresh look at dance and technology. Artistic director Wayne McGregor performs alongside his seven excellent dancers and collaborates with his award-winning design team. In Sulphur 16's white hot environment, space and time are distorted - forms fuse and melt, burn and mutate. Take your own trip through the performance, surf the sights and sounds and discover an experience which is yours alone.

Shobana Jeyasingh

a South Yorkshire Dance | Sheffield Theatres presentation

Shobana Jeyasingh's dance is unlike any other you're likely to see. She and her company of six dancers create and push dance in a whole new direction. 1999 sees the company celebrating its 10th anniversary with two new pieces. Memory and other Props sees Jeyasingh throwing caution and chronology to the wind as she explores the process of remembering by looking at dance she has created over the last 10 years and using elements of past works to create something unexpected and original. In Fine Frenzy Jeyasingh turns to the unpredictable jazz rhythms of Django Bates' music for her inspiration. The music will be performed live by the Apollo Saxophone Quartet.

Nederlands Dans Theater 2

a Sadler's Wells tour

Premiering new work by two of the world's leading choreographers, Jiri Kylian and Johan Ingar, with a repertoire of gravity-defying movement...the 14 young dancers bring a rare beauty to the stage. Awesomely physical and with professionalism that belies their years.

The Winter's Tale

written by William Shakespeare
directed by Declan Donellan
a Maly Drama Theatre of St. Petersburg production
performed in Russian with English surtitles

If you have seen the Maly before, you will need no persuading to book tickets for The Winter's Tale. If the Maly are new to you, don't miss this rare opportunity to experience this incredible company. A unique theatrical event combining Russian and British talent in a powerful production directed by a multi-award-winning team. The Winter's Tale is one of the most compelling and deeply moving of Shakespeare's plays. In less than a day, a deranged king throws his court into an oppressive darkness which lasts over twenty years. Innocent events become conspiracy and betrayal. Inexplicable rage leads to the renunciation of family and the very edge of madness.

Eugene Onegin

by Tchaikovsky
a Music Theatre London production

Tchaikovsky's moving tale of love, rejection, jealousy and murder is brought thrillingly to life in Tony Britten's brand new production. Amid the decayed splendour of the aristocracy, Eugene Onegin's cynicism breaks the heart of the woman who loves him. Only after he has killed his best friend does Onegin's bitterness turn to profound regret.

Die Fledermaus

by Strauss
a Music Theatre London production

This production of Strauss' enduringly popular opera is an opportunity to uncork another vintage MTL comedy. Fizzing with wit and topicality, this champagne fuelled celebration of Strauss' centenary bubbles with machination and mayhem.

Planted Seeds

choreographed by Darshan Singh Bhuller
a South Yorkshire Dance / Sheffield Theatres presentation

Inspired by British dancer / choreographer Darshan Singh Bhuller's first-hand experience of the war in former Yugoslavia, Planted Seeds recreates the true story of two young lovers - one Serb, one Muslim - and their desperate attempt to stay together. In a harrowing twist of fate the two were shot as they tried to cross the Sarajevo front line...set to the music of U2, Goran Bregovic, Yugoslavia's major pop star, and national folk tunes. **Planted Seeds** is performed by 6 outstanding dancers from three generations of British dance.

Wild Air

performed by the Siobhan Davies dance company
a South Yorkshire Dance/Sheffield Theatres presentation

Set to a specially commissioned score by celebrated composer Kevin Volans, **Wild Air** brings together Davies' multi award-winning company of dancers and regular team of collaborators to create a rich and evocative new dancework.

Angels in America Part One: Towards the Millennium

written by Tony Kushner
directed by Phil Willmott
a Sheffield Theatres production

Certain to shock, Towards the Millennium begins with a funeral and ends with a death, yet again and again its enormous energy and humour focus on survival and laughter. Directed by Phil Willmott, the play will be staged in a specially transformed Crucible - combining Studio-type intimacy with rich, exciting and spectacular design making full use of the Crucible's unique performing space. Tony Kushner's play is about this fragile earth, our fragile lives, heading towards the millennium on an epic journey through the dark underbelly of American life - full of corruption, forgotten losers and heartless winners.

A View from the Bridge

written by Arthur Miller
directed by Deborah Paige
a Sheffield Theatres production

Direct, vigorous and expressive, Arthur Miller's A View from the Bridge examines 'settling for half' - the point where our hopes, desires and sense of justice are compromised by relationships, pride and the law. New York's docks - a waterfront Wild West. In this place beyond the law, Eddie Carbone agrees to shelter his wife's cousins, Marco and Rodolpho, illegal immigrants from Sicily. It's not long before his wife's niece, Catherine, attracts the interest of the glamorous young Rodolpho. But does he love her, or the American citizenship a marriage to her would bring? Jealous and baffled, Eddie commits an unforgivable crime against his family and his community.

The Colour of Justice

The Stephen Lawrence Inquiry
edited by Richard Norton-Taylor
directed by Nicolas Kent with Surian Fletcher-Jones
a Tricycle Theatre production

Using a cast of 27 actors, this reconstruction examines the evidence from the moment Stephen Lawrence and Duwayne Brooks are attacked through the five years of the police investigation. It explores accusations of bungled investigation, corruption, and institutional racism in the Metropolitan police force. Nothing happens or is said on stage that did not take place at the Inquiry. The compelling story of the Lawrence family's search for justice and the failure of our society to bring Stephen's killers to justice.

One Flew Over the Cuckoo's Nest

adapted by Dale Wasserman from the novel by Ken Kesey
a Touring Consortium production

Life's not much fun at the State Mental Hospital under the iron rule of Nurse Ratched. But things are about to change. A new patient has arrived with an attitude that could blow the Institute of Psychology apart. As group therapy gives way to gambling, and parties take the place of pills and prayers, the maverick McMurphy is set on a collision course with the authorities. This hilarious and moving play is both a joyous celebration of human potential, and a deeply affecting ode to the outsider.

23:59

written by Nicola Baldwin
directed by Sarah Frankcom
a Sheffield Theatres production

A story of ambition and revenge in the music industry, set at the biggest party Sheffield's ever had. Will we make it to midnight? Find out at 23:59. Valentine, global pop icon, is in Sheffield to headline the millennium celebrations and look for local talent. Estelle, the woman who gave him his big break (and his best lyrics) plans to stop him. Can Valentine, voice of the 90s, talk his way out of this one? The clock's ticking - it's 23:59. Join Carol Cake, voice of the future, Cashpoint Lil and other clublife at the party to die for in the specially commissioned play, 23:59.

"Theatre is a basis for interpreting and enriching our lives. Emotional involvement in live performance benefits not only the artists but also the audience". See page 7